After the Heart of God

The Life and Ministry of Priests at the Beginning of the Third Millennium

JULIAN PORTEOUS

TAYLOR TRADE PUBLISHING

A CONNOR COURT BOOK
Lanham • New York • Boulder • Toronto • Plymouth, UK

Published by Taylor Trade Publishing
An imprint of The Rowman & Littlefield Publishing Group, Inc.
4501 Forbes Boulevard, Suite 200, Lanham, Maryland 20706
http://www.rlpgtrade.com

Estover Road, Plymouth PL6 7PY, United Kingdom

Distributed by National Book Network

British Library Cataloguing in Publication Information Available

Library of Congress Cataloging-in-Publication Data Available

ISBN 978-1-58979-579-2 (pbk. : alk. paper)
ISBN 978-1-58979-588-4 (electronic)

∞™ The paper used in this publication meets the minimum requirements of
American National Standard for Information Sciences—Permanence of Paper
for Printed Library Materials, ANSI/NISO Z39.48-1992.

Printed in the United States of America

Contents

Chapter One

Introduction

Yahweh has searched out a man for himself after his own heart and designated him leader of his people.[1]

The title for this book, *After the heart of God,* is taken from the account of the prophet Samuel selecting the one to be the next king of Israel. It is told in Chapter 16 of the First Book of Samuel. The prophet is sent to the sons of Jesse to anoint the one God has chosen. As he approaches the sons of Jesse he is struck by the eldest and assumes that this is the one. The prophet is told, "God does not see as man sees; man looks at appearances but Yahweh looks at the heart" (1 Sam16:7). Samuel examines the seven sons of Jesse and none is God's chosen one. Then the prophet asks the father, "Are these all the sons you have?" Jesse mentions that his youngest is not present as he is occupied looking after the sheep. He is sent for and the prophet identifies him as the one chosen by the Lord.

This fulfils a word given to Samuel: "Yahweh has searched out a man for himself after his own heart and designated him leader of his people" (1 Sam 13:14).

---

1 Sam 13:14

God calls men to the priesthood to be leaders of his people. God desires them to be men "after his own heart". The quality God desires most of all for those who are to be his priests is that they are men who are devoted to him with a singleness of mind and heart.

This book considers the type of priest God wants.

Priesthood in today's context

In the years since the Second Vatican Council the life and ministry of priests have been subject to many influences, influences both within and outside the Church, that have significantly affected the way the priesthood has been lived and exercised. It is important to consider some of the changes that have occurred. It is opportune to examine what is needed for the priesthood to move forward to meet the needs of the Church and the world as we enter the third Christian millennium.

Pope John Paul II commented in the introductory section to his Apostolic Exhortation *Pastores dabo vobis*:

> God always calls his priests from specific human and ecclesial contexts, which inevitably influence them; and to these same contexts the priest is sent for the service of Christ's Gospel. For this reason the synod desired to "contextualise" the subject of priests, viewing it in terms of today's society and today's Church in preparation for the third millennium.[2]

There is little doubt that the shape of priestly life and ministry is being moulded by a variety of factors from both within the Church and from the wider society. To reflect on the priesthood today this is a necessary point of departure. The priesthood, of course, does not change. It remains the one priesthood, the priesthood of Jesus

---

2 *Pastores dabo vobis*, n. 5.

Christ, but its expression is influenced by many factors that bear in on it. And the priesthood must adapt to the needs of the age. One could ask: what sort of priest is needed for these opening years of the third millennium?

Thoughts of a Seminary Rector

This book has emerged from a period of reflection on this question when, as Rector of the Seminary of the Good Shepherd in Sydney, Australia, this question came into sharp relief. As Rector it was important not just to presume on the past, but to look squarely at the reality of the "context" from which vocations today come and to which the newly ordained priests will be sent. It is also a question that the Church began asking itself in the light of factors that challenged the traditional identity of the priest. In the post-conciliar period the Church witnessed many priests struggling to come to terms with a changed social and ecclesial setting for their ministry. The question of the nature of the life and ministry of the priest became a matter of some real concern.

This book is a reflection on the times, and the needs of the Church and society. It is offered to priests to assist them in their reflection on their lives and ministry, and it is written in a particular way for seminarians as they look to their future service in the Church. It is hoped that this book will also assist lay people in understanding the nature and challenges of the priesthood at this moment in history.

Chapter Two

The social context

The world has changed much in the past forty years. There have been significant realignments in the political landscape of the world. The dominating issues in the 1960s now seem so distant as we look at what pre-occupies the world in the first decade of the third millennium. Society, particularly in Western First World countries, has changed quite dramatically. There has been unprecedented and accelerated change. We live in a world of change.

Australia has witnessed significant re-ordering of its social fabric. The cultural, moral and spiritual framework in which life in Australia is lived has evolved dramatically over the past four decades.

The context, "ad extra", in which the priesthood is now exercised, has been influenced by many factors. Some that deserve particular mention will be briefly explored. They are just a few of many that could be considered.

Secularisation

The processes of secularisation and the decline in practical participation in the life of the Church by many baptised Catholics are clearly evident to all thinking members of the Church. Priests who have exercised their ministry over the past forty years are only too aware of changes in the religious outlook of Catholics. We do not need to rehearse the figures that tell of significant decline in religious life in our nation. There has been a significant drop-off in attendance at Sunday Mass. There is a portion of those who could be called "the post-Vatican II generation" – those now in their fifties – who are alienated from the Church, wanting an institution more aligned with contemporary culture and contemporary attitudes to key moral issues. Many young people are quite oblivious to the Catholic faith; to them the Faith is irrelevant to their lives. The Church faces a real challenge in winning back its members to a real participation in its spiritual and sacramental life.

Priests see this daily in their parish ministry. Couples coming for Marriage, or presenting their children for Baptism, or families involved in the preparation of their children for First Holy Communion or Confirmation, want to receive the sacrament, but have no real intention of attending Mass regularly. The constant struggle with this issue can wear priests down so that they come to acquiesce to what is seen as the inevitable. This is not only demanding on the priest, but can be disheartening for his ministry. The priest can lose heart and come to his pastoral work with a simple human perspective, feeling at a loss to be able to communicate on the spiritual level. The people are simply not interested.

Individualism

Our age is an age of the individual. Personal rights, personal self-determination and individual freedom are regarded as absolutes by many. Along with this view has developed an attitude that each person is finally answerable only to himself. Acting according to one's "conscience" is considered the paramount right. It is commonly assumed that persons can form their own conscientious position on critical issues and are then free to follow what they have determined as right for them. In this world view relativism has flourished and many people resent any moral or spiritual authority interfering in what they view as their own sacrosanct domain. Many hold as a matter of absolute conviction the "primacy of conscience".

Priests experience this particularly when people make it clear to them that they do not accept that the Church can, as they would see it, dictate what they should believe and do. In fact priests can encounter a great deal of antagonism, even from practising Catholics, concerning the positions that the Church has adopted on certain moral and disciplinary issues. The issue that initiated this attitude is undoubtedly that of the teaching on birth control, but it now encompasses Church teaching on homosexuality, the role of women and bio-ethical issues. Many Catholics adopt the attitude that they can pick and choose what to accept in Church teaching.

Relativism

Many forces have combined to foster the view held by so many today that there are no longer any absolutes. The spirit of the age is that there is no absolute truth – there is "your truth" and "my truth". All things are seen to be in constant flux so that what we see today will be different tomorrow. There is the promotion of the subjective view of reality over the objective truth of things. People favour a plurality of opinion rather than the pursuit of what is right. Even religions are considered relative to one another: Christians have Christ, Muslims have the Prophet Mohammed, Hindus have Krishna. "We are all going the same way" is often the view about the comparative worth of the different religious traditions. According to this way of thinking the great sin is to be convinced about one's faith or religion, and thus viewed as a fundamentalist.

Pope Benedict has been a vocal critic of this "dictatorship of relativism". The words of the then Cardinal Ratzinger rang out at a Mass on 18 April 2005 just prior to the Conclave to elect the successor to Pope John Paul II. His words are worth offering here:

> How many winds of doctrine have we known in recent decades, how many ideological currents, how many ways of thinking. The small boat of the thought of many Christians has often been tossed about by these waves – flung from one extreme to another: from Marxism to liberalism, even to libertinism; from collectivism to radical individualism; from atheism to a vague religious mysticism; from agnosticism to syncretism and so forth. Every day new sects spring up, and what St Paul says about human deception and the trickery that strives to entice people into error (see Eph 4:14) comes true.
>
> Today, having a clear faith based on the Creed of the Church is often labelled as fundamentalism. Whereas relativism, that is, letting oneself be "tossed here and there, carried about by every wind of doctrine", seems the only attitude that can cope with modern times. We are building a dictatorship of relativism that does not recognise anything as definitive and whose ultimate goal consists solely of one's own ego and desires.[3]

This relativism has become all pervasive. The priest in the course of his pastoral work encounters this on a daily basis when people claim that there can be no definitive teachings, and the Church's position on any issue is seen as just one perspective, competing in the marketplace of ideas.

---

3 Mass "Pro eligendo romano pontifice", homily of his Eminence Cardinal Joseph Ratzinger, Dean of the College of Cardinals, 18 April 2005.

The spirit of democracy

Along with an emphasis on the rights of the individual goes a belief that societies are best governed by a democratic process. The "free world", led by the United States, actively campaigns for the establishment of democracy as the most just form of political life. The general experience is that democracy, despite all its faults, does ensure that those in political authority are accountable to the country that they govern. If an individual or party fails to meet the expectations of the people then they can be removed through the ballot box. The exercise of democracy does ensure that governments do not become self serving or seriously abuse power.

There is a growing chorus of voices that calls on the Church to embrace a more democratic form of government. Often the Church is viewed as a political organisation and authority is seen as the exercise of power. Such views often fail to see that the Church has been established by divine authority and is, according to its nature, hierarchical. Those critical of the Church's hierarchical structure often fail to appreciate that authority in the Christian dispensation is seen as an act of service, as the Lord so clearly taught[4].

Those who believe that the Church should become more democratic call for more participation in the decision-making processes at the local level through means of parish councils and diocesan councils and assemblies. Priests can sometimes find themselves under some pressure to allow for more "consultation"

---

4 Jesus taught and acted with authority. It was something people noticed about him (see Mk 1:22). However, he was most concerned to ensure that this authority was not used to his own advantage. He clearly saw that his role was to be one who served. He contrasted the way in which "worldly" authority was used and warned his disciples about the dangers of "lording it over people". He is Master and Lord (see Jn 13:13), yet he came as one who serves (see Mk 10:42) and one who was willing to lay down his life (ibid).

in their decision-making. Some parish councils can demand that matters be put to the vote, with the priest expected to accept the result. Those ascribing to the democratising of the Church often are critical of what they see as a clinging to clerical power. Priests can sometimes find it difficult to answer these charges.

Search for God – emergence of the New Age

Despite all the tendencies towards a secular way of life and the fact that many people live as "though God does not exist"[5], there is in evidence a search for the spiritual dimension of life. Often people who have rejected Christianity turn to esoteric spiritual teachings. This is firstly a challenge to us in the Church: how have we failed to show people the nature of the spiritual life and introduce people to the rich resource of spiritual teaching in the Church? And secondly it is an encouragement that despite all the attractions of a secular existence, deep within each person is a thirst for God and things of the spirit. The Apostolic Exhortation *Pastores dabo vobis*, expresses it thusly:

> The thirst for God and for an active meaningful relationship with him is so strong today that, where there is a lack of a genuine and full proclamation of the Gospel of Christ, there is a rising spread of forms of religiosity without God and the proliferation of many sects. For all children of the Church, and for priests especially, the increase of these phenomena, even in some traditionally Christian environments, is not only a constant motive to examine our consciences as to the credibility of our witness to the Gospel but at the same time is a sign of how deep and widespread is the search for God.[6]

---

5 See Pope John Paul II, Apostolic Exhortation, *Christifideles Laici*, n. 34.
6 Pope John Paul II, Apostolic Exhortation, *Pastores dabo vobis*, n. 6.

The profusion of forms of spirituality drawing on ancient pagan cults will be a passing phenomenon, taking the shape of "fads", but they are a challenge to the Church. We have the experience and the wisdom concerning the spiritual life and yet have failed to communicate it.

The Changing Ethnic Face of Australian life

On a completely different level, it is worth commenting upon the effect of the migration patterns on the life of the Church. Since the end of the Second World War there have been waves of migration to Australia. Beginning with European migrants, we have seen successive waves of migrants from countries that have experienced particular difficulties, e.g., Lebanon, the Philippines, Vietnam, and now the Middle East. The Church has benefited from the fact that many of the groups that have migrated have contained significant proportions of Catholics and it has led to the contribution of their traditions to the life of the Church in Australia. It has also meant that the Catholic Church has now become the largest religious body in Australia.

The face of the Church has significantly changed from its Anglo-Celtic character to being richly multicultural. In the larger urban centres it is the migrant communities that have become a major presence in our Sunday Masses.

Along with the changing ethnic face of the Church in Australia has gone the changing face of the clergy. In recent years, increasingly because of a need to provide a supply of priests for parish ministry, the presence of priests from different ethnic origins is becoming a feature of the face of the priesthood. In the larger urban dioceses priests from diverse cultures make up a significant proportion of the diocesan clergy. While many priests from different cultural backgrounds have enriched the life of the Church, it has not been without difficulties. The issue of pronunciation of English is one immediate issue. Sometimes the priest cannot be clearly understood and this can be quite frustrating for Anglo-Celtic Australian parishioners. A second issue is that some priests do not have sufficient grasp of the culture of the Church in Australia and sometimes do not engage well with parishioners, or are unable to be as pastorally effective as they should be.

Role of women

Other issues have smouldered in society and have impacted on the Church. The question of the role of women in society has been a significant issue since the early days of the "feminist" movement. The quest for legal and financial equality for women and the right of women to exercise a greater role in society has been a steady question in society over the past thirty years. Many significant social changes have been wrought. Women are now very active in the workplace, and some have risen to positions of considerable standing in politics and industry.

The issue has been felt in the Church in two areas in particular: one revolved around the use of "inclusive" language, especially in the Liturgy. Some object to the use of the word "man" to depict humanity and object to the masculine pronoun being used of God. Charges of "sexist" are levelled at priests who do not conform to modern sensibilities. Despite the Vatican producing *Liturgiam authenticam*[7] outlining its principles for authentic translation of liturgical texts, there is still strong opinion among some that the Church is not alert to modern sensibilities.

The second issue concerns the call for greater participation of women in the governing structures of the Church. The latter question has prompted repeated challenging of the Church's view that the priesthood is only open to men. Despite the

---

7 *Liturgiam authenticam,* On the use of vernacular languages in the publication of the Books of the Roman Liturgy, 7 May 2001.

Church firmly teaching the equal dignity of women,[8] there has remained an underlying disquiet among some women that they are discriminated against in the Church. Equality is seen as sameness and the notion of the complementary nature of the roles of men and women is often not accepted.

Marriage and Family

The significant social changes over the past forty years have had an impact on marriage and family life. Many young people are preferring to enter into marriage at an older age (often influenced by the desire of women to develop a career) and cohabitation has become a widespread phenomenon. Priests are faced with the fact that the vast majority of young couples who approach them to be married have been cohabiting and have no sense of this being inappropriate.

Modern couples have largely embraced a "contraceptive mentality", and simply cannot grasp the Church's position on the use of contraceptives.

Marriages are less stable as rates of divorce have increased. There are many Catholics living in a second marriage, and, not having sought an annulment of the first marriage, have married outside the Church. This creates issues in relation to participating fully in the life of the Church.

Marriage and family life are under stress from many factors – from mortgage pressures to efforts to juggle work and family responsibilities. Children are affected by lack of stability in family life.

A priest working in a parish experiences the difficulties facing marriages and families in all these ways. He finds it difficult to convey the full Christian vision of marriage and family.

---

8 See *Mulieris dignitatem* (1988), *Letter to Women* (1995).

The gay-rights movement

We have witnessed the rise of the "gay-rights movement" over the last thirty years. Those in the movement have sought to change the attitude of society towards the practice of homosexuality. It has become a potent social force demanding more and more rights, and insisting on a recognition of the legitimacy of its lifestyle. The movement has achieved significant legislative changes, and actively promotes homosexuality as an equal alternative to heterosexuality. From the annual "Mardi Gras" through Sydney streets to the rewriting of text books for children, this movement has been very effective in gaining the support of many Catholics for its objectives.

The traditional teaching of the Church on the question of the morality of active homosexuality, captured succinctly in the *Catechism of the Catholic Church*[9], has characterised the Church in the eyes of those active in the movement as a major threat to their agenda. Within the Church some have been agitating for acceptance of the homosexual lifestyle. This has been typified in the "Rainbow Sash" incidents with Cardinal Pell at both St Patrick's Cathedral, Melbourne and St Mary's Cathedral, Sydney.[10]

The Church has suffered through a homosexual sub-culture penetrating seminaries in the 1970s.[11] The clerical sexual abuse crisis which emerged in recent years was caused in no small part by the

---

9 See *Catechism of the Catholic Church (CCC)*, pars. 2357-59.
10 Cardinal Pell as the then Archbishop of Melbourne, and later as Archbishop of Sydney, did not give Holy Communion to self-declared practising homosexuals who appeared on Pentecost Sunday at St Patrick's Cathedral, Melbourne, and at St Mary's Cathedral, Sydney, subsequently, wearing rainbow sashes and requesting communion. Rather than giving communion, Cardinal Pell offered blessings, which were refused by some. "Anybody who is sinning seriously should not go to communion", he said in 2001. "So a gay person who has repented, or a gay person who is not active, is more than welcome to communion."
11 See Michael S. Rose, *Goodbye, Good Men*, Aquinas Publishing, 2002.

presence of a subculture of homosexuality in the priesthood.[12]

An emerging issue related to the "gay-rights" movement is the pressure being applied to civil authority to recognise same-sex unions as an alternative to marriage between a man and woman. They are insisting on challenging the traditional view on the nature of marriage. This will have far reaching consequences for the future of society.[13]

The Church's position on homosexuality, spelt out in the *Catechism of the Catholic Church* and in the document of the Congregation for the Doctrine of the Faith, *Letter to the Bishops of the Catholic Church on the pastoral care of homosexual persons* (1986), has been subject to strong criticism and the accusation of being "homophobic". The Church has sought to retain a pastoral concern for the spiritual and moral wellbeing of the individual while stating clearly:

> The Church, obedient to the Lord who founded her and gave to her the sacramental life, celebrates the divine plan of the loving and live-giving union of men and women in the sacrament of marriage. It is only in the marital relationship that the use of the sexual faculty can be morally good. A person engaging in homosexual behaviour therefore acts immorally.[14]

The Church's position has been often misquoted and misrepresented, particularly in the popular media. Despite strong opposition, the priest is challenged to teach the position of the Church faithfully while maintaining a pastoral sensitivity – a great challenge in the current climate. As the Instruction states, "Christians who are homosexual are called, as all of us are, to a chaste life. As they dedicate their lives to understanding the nature

---

12 This view is argued by a number of authors. See *Goodbye, Good Men.*
13 See Dale O'Leary, *One Man, One Woman*, Sophia Institute Press, 2007.
14 Congregation for the Doctrine of the Faith, *Letter to the Bishops of the Catholic Church on the pastoral care of homosexual persons* (1986), n. 7.

of God's personal call to them, they will be able to celebrate the Sacrament of Penance more faithfully and receive the Lord's grace so freely offered there in order to convert their lives more fully to his Way".[15]

Ethical "hot buttons" and social issues

Another important development in our time has been the remarkable advances in bio-technology. Ethical questions surrounding IVF (in-vitro fertilisation) and embryo stem cell research and cloning have been vigorously debated, and the Catholic Church has had an active voice. Legislative changes at both national and state level have largely allowed these procedures to be approved, despite strong objection from the Church.

An issue bubbling below the surface in society is the morality of euthanasia. While a referendum succeeded in achieving a "No" vote, there is still pressure in some quarters to allow its introduction. It will remain an issue for the Church to contend with.

Australian society is struggling to make any headway in the fight against the obvious dangers of the use of recreational drugs. Earlier issues surrounding smoking marihuana, and the use of heroin and cocaine have now moved to the wide usage of amphetamines and "recreational drugs" like "ice", particularly associated with the dance scene. More recently concern has been raised about "binge drinking" among young people.

Australian society faces a number of significant challenges to ensure that the social fabric does not unravel. The Church has a vital role to play in society. Through the ministry of priests the wisdom of the tradition of Catholic faith and morality can be imparted to "the faithful". The Church, too, needs to maintain a voice "in the marketplace".

---

15 *ibid.*, n. 12.

The contemporary context

This is the world and society experienced in Australia in the first decades of the third millennium. This is the context in which a priest is to exercise his ministry. All these influences and many others as well touch the daily life of the members of the Church. Society is in continuous flux and a vast array of political, social, cultural and moral forces are constantly at work shaping the future direction that Australian society will take.

A priest carries out his ministry within this ever changing context. A priest is aware of the many forces that shape the views and attitudes of the people he serves. He brings the Word of God expressed in the Scriptures, the living Tradition of the Church and his own personal experience of faith to bear in ministering as a priest in the midst of contemporary society.

A priest, particularly a priest ministering in a parish, lives in close contact with the society around him and is acutely aware of the power and influence of the many streams of thought and attitude upon the lives of the people he serves. He sees first hand how these influences shape for better or worse the lives of his people.

This is the "social context" in which the priest ministers today.

Chapter Three

The ecclesial context

Within the Church there has been a period of significant change over the past forty years. Again, the main lines of change are well known. We will consider some of the changes that have shaped the life and direction of the Church over the past forty years.

The Celebration of the Liturgy

The significant recasting of the form of our worship has had a profound effect in the Church. The emphasis has been upon the participation of people in the liturgical action, inspired by the teaching of the Constitution on the Liturgy, *Sacrosanctum Concilium* urging "full and active participation"[16] by the people in the Sacred Liturgy. One not necessarily intended result of this has been that at the parish level the liturgy has become more "horizontal" with an emphasis on community participation. At a popular level there is a tendency to see the liturgy as a means to commemorate persons and events in the life of the community. This is often testified to at a funeral Mass when the funeral rite is described as "a celebration of the life of.....". Liturgy as an act of worship of

---

16 "Mother Church earnestly desires that all the faithful should be led to that fully conscious and active participation in liturgical celebrations which is demanded by the very nature of the liturgy." (*Sacrosanctum Concilium*, n. 14).

God has retreated to the background of people's understanding. This is evidenced in the more popular sense that the Mass is a community meal rather than a representation of the sacrifice of Christ on the Cross.

Facing the people for the celebration of the Mass has challenged priests to be more personally engaged with the people. Sometimes this has gone to extremes as priests have tried to be overly familiar and jocular. It has greatly affected the way in which priests celebrate Mass. Often too, the need for a range of lay ministries for the Mass puts pressure on the priest as last minute organisation prevents him from quietly and prayerfully preparing for the celebration of the Sacred Mysteries. Mass can become more of a performance for priest and people. The effectiveness of the Mass is often assessed according to how well it was received by the people.

We have witnessed a significant change in the style of music used in the Liturgy: it has become more "popular" and contemporary. One rarely hears music composed before the Second Vatican Council. The rich tradition of Latin hymns and Mass settings is deemed inappropriate for the contemporary style of liturgical celebration. Congregational singing has developed while the role of a choir has diminished.

Questions concerning the celebration of the Liturgy continue to dog priests at the parish level. There is the issue of the translation of the normative Latin text into English. The process of a fresh translation is proving a long drawn out affair. Some are strongly of the view that inclusive language is culturally necessary today and when the new translation of the liturgical texts is finally produced there will be not a few disappointed with the result.

The "Old Rite"

The question of language also involves the use of Latin in the liturgy. The vast bulk of priests and people now accept and prefer a vernacular liturgy but there is a small, determined group of Catholics who wish to participate in the "Old Rite", the Tridentine Mass. Recent relaxation of restrictions on its use by Pope Benedict[17] has encouraged some to want it made even more available. Interestingly, there is a significant number of young people who have never known the liturgy as it was celebrated prior to the changes brought about by Vatican II who are attracted to this rite. Some voices are now being raised in favour of a return to the "Ad Orientem"[18] way of celebrating Mass.

The celebration of the Liturgy is at the heart of the life and ministry of priests. The adage, "Lex orandi, lex credendi" (the law of prayer is the law of faith) is true in a particular way for priests whose spirituality has been traditionally understood to emanate from the liturgy. How the liturgy is celebrated deeply influences the way the priest views himself and his ministry.

Re-ordering of churches

One of the contentious issues in the years after the Second Vatican Council was the "re-ordering of churches" to fit in with what was perceived as the new requirements for the celebration of the Liturgy. At times these re-orderings were accompanied by a good degree of angst among the people – the removal of altar rails and statues, occasionally the demolition of high altars, the

---

17 Pope Benedict XVI decreed, "The Roman Missal promulgated by Paul VI is the ordinary expression of the 'Lex orandi' (Law of prayer) of the Catholic Church of the Latin rite. Nonetheless, the Roman Missal promulgated by St. Pius V and reissued by Bl. John XXIII is to be considered as an extraordinary expression of that same 'Lex orandi,' and must be given due honour for its venerable and ancient usage. These two expressions of the Church's Lex orandi will in no any way lead to a division in the Church's 'Lex credendi' (Law of belief). They are, in fact two usages of the one Roman rite. It is, therefore, permissible to celebrate the Sacrifice of the Mass following the typical edition of the Roman Missal promulgated by Bl. John XXIII in 1962 and never abrogated, as an extraordinary form of the Liturgy of the Church". (Art 1, Apostolic Letter, "*Summorum Pontificum*," made public at the Vatican July 7, 2007).

18 *Ad Orientem* means "to the East" and reflects the ancient custom of the Church of celebrating the Mass facing the East, the place of the rising sun, with priest and people facing the same direction, the position popularly called "back to the people".

orienting of the altar and tabernacle to a side position, and so on. The prevailing attitude was to "simplify" the interiors and remove all the accretions of the past.

New designs for churches were developed in the years after the Council. The focus of the architecture was to provide the possibility for people to gather around the altar. A fan shape replaced the rectangular or cruciform pattern. In keeping with contemporary architectural styles churches were "minimalist" and generally monochrome in colour. Churches often looked less like churches from the outside as well.

The defining feature of more recent expressions of church design has been a focus on making the church building "people friendly". A term like "gathering space" reflects a mentality that a church should firstly consider the needs of the people. The emphasis here is on the community. The notion of the "house of God" has receded into the background. The replacement of pews with plastic individual seating, the "multi-purpose" building that was the fashion at one time, the placing of the tabernacle on a side altar or in a separate room, all confirm this tendency. The sense Catholics have had of the Church as a sacred place for worship and prayer has been replaced with a functionality focused on the community. Churches, once imbued with a sense of holy silence, now resound to chatter and milling around.

History will judge this post-Conciliar period of church architecture. Already there is an emerging critique that argues that this period has depleted the cultural heritage of church architecture. The next period may see a return to the design of churches which more richly captures the spiritual and devotional heritage of the Church.

For priests this has been a difficult period. Some have embraced the new approach seen as reflecting the "spirit of Vatican II". Others have wanted to preserve the more traditional styles of church design. Whatever the position of the priest, he finds himself being challenged by some of the opposing view.

Clerical sexual abuse

The year 2002 was an "annus horribilis" for priests. On January 6 the *Boston Globe* exposed the fact that a former priest, John Geoghan, had abused as many as 130 boys over a thirty year period. The issue was not just that a priest who was given the title "Father" and who had a privileged place in the lives of the Catholic faithful had been guilty of a gross misuse of his role in the sexual abuse of minors, but that the crime was known about by his superiors and he was allowed to move from parish to parish over this extended period. There was a twofold issue here: that of a priest so seriously harming those entrusted to his pastoral care, and the serious failure of his bishop to act to protect young men from his predatory behaviour.

This revelation sparked a process whereby more and more information about priests abusing young people came to light. The media exposed case after case not only in Boston, but in a large number of dioceses across the United States. Priests were named. Many priests still exercising pastoral roles were forced to resign. Lawsuits ran into tens of millions of dollars. Some dioceses were forced into bankruptcy.

The issue did not stay in the United States, it spread to England and Ireland and to Australia. It was a most difficult time for the Church. Lay people were scandalised, not only by the behaviour of priests, but many felt let down by their bishops. The Church came under intense media scrutiny. Governments began investigations. New laws were enacted requiring careful scrutiny of any priest whose ministry involves young people. The Church was severely damaged by the revelations. The priesthood was placed under a cloud.

Priests suffered much during this period. Some came under

personal attack and insult. Others felt betrayed by their brothers in the priesthood as all priests came under a blanket of suspicion. Priests, who before enjoyed respect and trust among Catholics and in the general community, now experienced a vulnerability. A claim could be made against a priest and he had little redress. He was required to stand aside from his ministry. There were a number of false claims made against some priests, and they discovered that their capacity to declare their innocence was very limited. Protocols were developed which tended to be weighted towards the victims. Still today the processes involving priests and claims of sexual abuse are unsatisfactory.

Priests have suffered much during this period.

Decline in Vocations

A particular reality which has occupied the minds of priests and bishops in recent years is the decline in vocations to the priesthood. The fewer men coming forward as priests has meant that there are now lesser numbers of priests in most Australian dioceses and the clergy are aging. This is a matter of major concern as parishes which previously had two or more priests now have one. Most priests now live alone. More and more priests are being asked to take on extra responsibilities – parishes are being "partnered" as two or more parish communities are being overseen by one parish priest. There is no end in sight and all predictions suggest a serious lack of priests to provide even the most basic services. Country dioceses are likely to be the places where this lack of priests will be most keenly felt.

The lack of assistant priests means that all the tasks required in the parish are now falling to the one priest – sacramental preparation, liturgical preparation, State School catechesis, youth ministry. Whereas once a parish priest could delegate these sorts of roles to his curate, now they fall on his shoulders. Many priests are now assisted by lay people to meet these demands, but the burden is more keenly felt by the priests.

This issue is one that has evoked wide discussion within the Church. There are many who believe that the Church needs to change its discipline in regard to the demand for a celibate clergy.

There are some signs that more young men are coming forward to embrace a priestly vocation. Vocations world-wide have increased significantly. At the Seminary of the Good Shepherd, Sydney, the number of seminarians has doubled in the past seven years. However rates of ordination are still not where they need to be and it is clearly evident that in the foreseeable future there will be a serious shortage of priests in dioceses in Australia.

Many dioceses have turned to inviting priests from other countries to come and serve in Australia. This has been met with a mixed response from people and priests. One of the key concerns is that foreign born priests can lack a level of spoken English that can be clearly understood, and there is a concern that priests coming to Australia lack a cultural awareness.

This is placing a burden on priests. They are being asked to do more. They are getting older. They do not see any solution on the horizon.

Changing role of Religious

We have noticed also a significant change in the role of religious in the Church. They have moved out of many of their traditional roles, for instance, in education and health and have taken on new forms of service within the Church in areas like social justice, spirituality and pastoral roles. They have largely abandoned their traditional form of life and have opted for more secular forms of dress. Along the way the numbers of religious have declined significantly and a number of orders anticipate their passing into history.

The changing mode of presence of religious in the Church has had a particular effect on the life of priests. Often in the past the religious carried out a complementary role to that of the priest in the local parish. The small community of sisters conducted the parish primary school and assisted in the preparation of children for the sacraments. The sisters often contributed to the celebration of the liturgy in various ways. The sisters carried out their own pastoral role with families and the poor. This has all but disappeared.

The "good sisters" often provided a personal support for the priest. They, like him, were dedicated to the people of the parish. Particularly in isolated rural parishes the relationship between the priest and the religious was mutually nourishing at a personal level. Now the priest is alone.

Emergence of the role of the lay person

The declining and changing place of religious in the life of the Church was first keenly felt in education. Religious had been the backbone of a remarkable story of the Church investing itself in providing Catholic education for its children. From having the generous dedication of religious in Catholic education for over one century we now look to lay teachers to continue the great tradition of Catholic education. A simple expression of this is that in 1965 there were 668 religious and no lay persons as principals in Catholic schools. In 2006 there were just 48 religious principals and 537 lay principals. What occurred in Catholic schools was replicated in Catholic hospitals.

The shape of parish life has significantly altered as lay people step forward to assume a vast variety of roles in enabling the parish to carry out its functions. While we are witnessing a growing number of lay people being employed in forms of pastoral work in parishes, it is the vast army of volunteers that now carry so much of the daily work and service in parishes.

The engagement of lay people in so many of the works of the

parish has been a wonderful thing. Priests now rely upon them very much. Lay people themselves have developed a stronger tie to the parish and the priest. Often this has led to closer and more personal relationships between the priest and parishioners. This has been a good thing.

Catholic Schools

The transition from Catholic schools as the work of Religious Orders to the present reality of Catholic schools being principally conducted by lay people has been a great success. There has been largely a smooth transition and dedicated and competent lay teachers have enabled schools to continue to function and indeed to flourish. Catholic schools are highly sought after not only by Catholic parents but by many parents who see the Catholic school as providing a superior level of education.

Catholic schools are recognised as providing a high quality of education. They have excelled in some aspects of the human formation of students,[19] but there are some serious concerns about the ability of Catholic schools to adequately ensure an effective transmission of the faith.

In 2007 the bishops of NSW and ACT produced a pastoral letter on Catholic Schools entitled *Catholic Schools at a Crossroads*. The central thrust of the document is the concern of the bishops that Catholic schools:

- are truly Catholic in their identity and life
- are centres of "the new evangelisation"
- enable our students to achieve high levels of "Catholic religious literacy" and practice
- are led and staffed by people who will contribute to these goals[20]

The letter of the bishops echoes the concern of many priests who

---

19 Catholic Schools are renowned for the quality of the pastoral care of students. Schools seek to foster an altruistic spirit and many students have a keen social conscience.
20 Summary, *Catholic Schools at a Crossroads*, p. 3.

witness that despite a comprehensive Catholic education students have not being active participants in parish life. There is currently a single digit percentage of Mass attendance by young people leaving our Catholic schools.

The impact of the ecclesial context on priests

It is true to say that priests have found the ecclesial context for their ministry one that has been a source of much challenge and often insufficient support. The more united and structurally sound ecclesial context of past years is no longer in evidence. There are many cracks in the system. Priests find themselves more isolated and exposed in their pastoral efforts. They are feeling the strain!

There are however signs of hope for the future.

Chapter Four

Signs of new life

The landscape of the Church over the last quarter century has been dominated by the figure of Pope John Paul II, whose twenty six and a half year reign has not only been significant in terms of its length but more particularly by its impact. People have been referring to him as "John Paul the Great". His influence on the Church and on world events during the time of his pontificate has been extraordinary. It is difficult to adequately catalogue all his achievements.

Influence of Pope John Paul II

The first most evident aspect of his influence was his drive to make immediate contact with people. He made 104 pastoral visits, or "pilgrimages" as he liked to call them, to countries across the world. In the course of his 1,160 Wednesday audiences he spoke to some 17.6 million pilgrims. Pope John Paul became the most visible and well known of any pope in history. He brought a dynamic presence of the Church not only into Catholic life, but to world events.

When he became pope in 1978 he set about giving definition to the teaching of the Second Vatican Council. There had been a period of dispute over the way the teaching of the Council was to be interpreted. The phrase, "spirit of Vatican II", came to be the catch cry for those who sought to bring innovation inspired, as they believed, by the intentions of the fathers of the Council. Many times Pope John Paul would refer back to conciliar documents and provide an authoritative interpretation of the teaching of the Council in which he had been a contributor.

A body of teaching

As well as intending to confirm the faith of Catholics in the midst of many complex issues that occupied the Church internally, a central theme of the Pope's teaching was to propose a path for the Church as an active and positive agent in society. Pope John Paul did not see the Church as retreating from the issues that were shaping social and cultural life. His first encyclical *Redemptor Hominis* (1979) set this agenda as he presented a Christian anthropology which was to be the basis of much of his moral teaching. His encyclicals addressed issues concerning human life. For instance, in the Apostolic Exhortation *Familiaris Consortio* (1981) he explored the nature and role of the family; in *Mulieris Dignitatem* (1988) he addressed the highly debated question of the dignity and role of women in society and the Church; in *Christifideles Laici* (1988) he broke new ground in an understanding of the role of the lay person in the Church and reaffirmed the critical role the lay person has in secular events; in *Evangelium Vitae* (1995) he spoke passionately on the question of respect for human life. His rich Christian anthropology also provided a basis for his several encyclicals on the social teaching of the Church: in *Laborem Exercens* (1981) he taught on the dignity of human work; in *Solicitudo Rei Socialis* (1987) on issues concerning development in the Third Word; and in *Centesimus Annus* (1991) while providing a commentary on both socialism and capitalism he returned to his central theme of the transcendent dignity of the human person.

He also wrote two great encyclicals on key intellectual issues that were debated both in society and in the Church. In *Veritatis Splendor* (1993) he addressed the nature of moral thinking and in *Fides et Ratio* (1998) he defended the capacity of human beings to know objective truth. Both these encyclicals promoted a great deal of discussion not only among Catholic theologians but also among secular thinkers who responded to his proposals.

The body of teaching by the Pope helped foster a renewed theological effort, and encouraged a group of young theologians to present with a fresh vitality the tradition of Catholic thought. Nowhere was this more evident than in a series of 129 Wednesday catecheses on human sexuality, which became known as "the Theology of the Body". This detailed and carefully argued presentation of a Catholic view on sexuality stimulated a significant body of literature as theologians addressed with renewed vigour one of the pressing questions of our time – the nature and place of sexuality in human life. One outcome of this was the establishing of the John Paul II Institutes for Marriage and the Family, now established in several centres across the world.

New movements

During his long pontificate the Pope witnessed the emergence of a range of spiritual movements particularly among the laity, many of which took highly structured forms. As the phenomenon developed, the Pope engaged directly with these movements establishing relationships with them and calling them into the heart of the Church. These movements came to be called "ecclesial movements" because they embraced not only lay people but priests and consecrated people as well, indeed becoming a source of vocations to the priesthood and consecrated life.

Some movements like Focolare, L'Arche, Neo Catechumenal Way and Communio e Liberazione had in fact been founded prior to Vatican II, but they flourished in the post Vatican II environment. Other movements emerged in the 1960s and 1970s. Many were inspired by the Charismatic Renewal and focused on a personal experience of the Holy Spirit and the exercise of spiritual gifts. The grace associated with the experience of the Holy Spirit was expressed in prayer meetings, but later this grace inspired the development of communities structured around weekly gatherings and under centralised leadership. A number of these communities now boast a membership in the thousands, and have become international in their scope.

Pope John Paul called these communities together on Pentecost Sunday, 1998. Half a million people gathered in St Peter's Square and spilled out down as far as the Tiber. The Pope on this occasion confirmed that their charisms were acknowledged by the Church and he encouraged them to work closely with the hierarchy of the Church. In an extraordinarily positive and hopeful address the Pope said in part:

> Today the Church rejoices at the renewed confirmation of the prophet Joel's words which we have just heard: "I will pour out my Spirit upon all flesh" (Acts 2:17). You, present here, are the tangible proof of this "outpouring" of the Spirit. Each movement is different from the others, but they are all united in the same communion and for the same mission. Some charisms given by the Spirit burst in like an impetuous wind, which seizes people and carries them to new ways of missionary commitment to the radical service of the Gospel, by ceaselessly proclaiming the truths of faith, accepting the living stream of tradition as a gift and instilling in each person an ardent desire for holiness.
>
> Today, I would like to cry out to all of you gathered here in St Peter's Square and to all Christians: Open yourselves docilely to the gifts of the Spirit! Accept

gratefully and obediently the charisms which the Spirit never ceases to bestow on us! Do not forget that every charism is given for the common good, that is, for the benefit of the whole Church.[21]

Pope John Paul moved with great conviction to affirm the place and role of the movements in the future of the Church.

A New Evangelisation

Earlier Pope Paul VI had left the Church a great legacy in his milestone document, *Evangelii Nuntiandi* (1975), following the Synod of bishops which met in 1974 at the Pope's behest to discuss the subject of evangelisation. In this encyclical the Pope had declared in clear and bold terms: "Evangelisation is in fact the grace and vocation proper to the Church, her deepest identity. She exists in order to evangelise".[22]

Then at the beginning of his pontificate (1979) Pope John Paul took part in a General Conference of Latin American Bishops held at Puebla, Mexico. The theme was evangelisation in Latin America. Against a background of "Liberation Theology" – a controversial question at that time in Latin America – Pope John Paul spoke about evangelisation not being reduced to a temporal project but being about transforming the human heart. A transformed heart will be the source of a transformed culture, creating what he described as a "civilisation of love".

In 1983 the Pope first spoke of something that was to become a constant in his teaching over the next 20 years: the "New Evangelisation". He first mentioned it at Haiti in relation to the 500th anniversary of the first evangelisation of Latin America with the arrival of the Europeans. The Pope stated that a "new" evangelisation was needed in countries and societies which had

---

21 World congress of ecclesial movements and new communities, Pentecost 1998, n. 5.
22 *Evangelii Nuntiandi*, n. 14.

been evangelised in past times but have now lost the vigour of faith. The Pope saw that they needed to receive the Gospel afresh. He spoke again and again of the need to bring a revitalised message of salvation to civilisations that were formally Christian, but are now suffering under a loss of faith and a growing secularism.

His Apostolic Exhortation, *Christifideles Laici* (1988) recapitulates the ideas expressed on various occasions and in various places. In a section entitled: *The Hour Has Come for a Re-Evangelisation*, the Pope states:

> Whole countries and nations where religion and the Christian life were formerly flourishing and capable of fostering a viable and working community of faith, are now put to a hard test, and in some cases, are even undergoing a radical transformation, as a result of a constant spreading of an indifference to religion, of secularism and atheism. This particularly concerns countries and nations of the so-called First World, in which economic well-being and consumerism, even if coexistent with a tragic situation of poverty and misery, inspires and sustains a life lived "as if God did not exist".[23]

In *Redemptoris Missio* (1990) the Pope spoke of the evangelising mission of the Church and called on the Church to commit itself to the work of evangelisation. He distinguished between the first evangelisation to those who have never heard the Gospel and the need to proclaim the Gospel anew in areas where secularism has drained the faith of large groups of people:

> In countries with ancient Christian roots, and occasionally in the younger Churches as well, entire groups of the baptised have lost a living sense of the

23 *Christifideles Laici*, n. 34.

faith or even no longer consider themselves members of the Church and live a life far removed from Christ and his Gospel. In this case what is needed is a 'new evangelisation' or a 're-evangelisation'.[24]

This call to the Church was a constant theme of Pope John Paul. Priests in countries like Australia which are experiencing the serious inroads of secularism are urged to re-think their ministry now in terms of engaging in the task of the new evangelisation. We will return to this question later in the book.

An apostle to youth

The Pope showed great confidence not only in the new movements about which some pastors within the Church were hesitant, but he particularly looked to the young as being a key to the future of the Church. At a time when many young people were disenchanted with "organised religion" the Pope, building on his experience in Poland as a young priest, reached out to youth. He had the capacity not only to engage with youth, but he revealed that he had great confidence in them. He understood that young people have a willingness to aspire to noble ideals and the Pope presented them with the most noble of causes: to be saints!

He called young people to meet with him in St Peter's Square on Palm Sunday 1984. Three hundred thousand assembled and from that moment the Pope sought to hold an annual "world youth day". These meetings with young people quickly came to be held in different locations across the world: Argentina, Spain, North America, Philippines, Poland, France, Germany and Australia. They grew in size and significance. They have become the largest gatherings of young people in the world. More importantly they have given birth to a generation of young Catholics who have

---

24 *Redemptoris Missio*, n. 33.

a deep love for their Catholic faith and see themselves being ambassadors for the pope's vision of a "new civilisation of love"[25], rebuilding human society based on Christian principles.

The phenomenon of World Youth Days is clear testimony to the fact that the Church has the capacity to communicate with and engage the energies of the young. Priests who struggle to find ways to effectively minister to youth can take great heart from this. The Church can inspire and rally young people to its life and mission.

Entering the new millennium

All these elements listed above have shaped the nature of the Church as it now is. While we can honestly acknowledge many problems and challenges, it is also clear that there are many encouraging signs, signs of hope. A particular focus for Pope John Paul was the celebration of the year 2000 and the entry of the Church into the third millennium. He wrote two documents, one leading up to the year 2000 (*Tertio Millennio Adveniente*, 1994) and one as the new millennium began (*Novo Millennio Ineunte*, 2000). The second of these two letters offered an inspiring call to the Church to go out

---

25 This notion was a common theme in the writings and preaching of Pope John Paul II. He acknowledges that the phrase belongs to Pope Paul VI (see *Sollicitudo Rei Socialis*, n. 33). It was his call to the youth of the World at Denver 1993 and was a key theme in his encyclical, *Evangelium Vitae*, 1995. He said to the youth at Denver, "At this stage of history, the liberating message of the Gospel of life has been put into your hands. And the mission of proclaiming it to the ends of the earth is now passing to your generation. Like the great apostle Paul, you too must feel the full urgency of the task: "Woe to me if I do not evangelise" (1 Cor 9:16). Woe to you if you do not succeed in defending life. The church needs your energies, your enthusiasm, your youthful ideals, in order to make the Gospel of life penetrate the fabric of society, transforming people's hearts and the structures of society in order to create a civilisation of true justice and love. Now more than ever, in a world that is often without light and without the courage of noble ideals, people need the fresh, vital spirituality of the Gospel".

into the deep ("duc in altum"). In other words, the Pope, himself now old and feeling his age, called on the Church to look to the future with confidence and embrace it with purpose. He spoke of a "new springtime for the Church".[26]

A New Pope

The choice of Cardinal Ratzinger as Pope to follow John Paul II was received surprise by many and cautious support from those who were hoping for a new era with a more "progressive" spirit. While clearly his own man, Pope Benedict continues the legacy of Pope John Paul II.

He expresses a clear sense of mission for the Church in facing the challenges of a moral relativism infecting Western societies. It is evident that under the leadership of Benedict the Church will continue to move forward with a confident sense of its role and mission in the modern world.

Priests can approach their challenging mission "at the coalface" knowing that the Church at its centre has a clear and purposeful agenda. The priest can be assured that his efforts to bring the Gospel and the teaching of the Church to bear on the lives of people living in the midst of the world will be supported by a teaching office that is in touch with the realities of the contemporary world and will speak to the challenges of the time.

---

26 The theme of "the new springtime" for the Church became a familiar one in a number of later writings of the Pope. One particular reference was in his meetings with the movements in May 1998 where he spoke of the movements as a hope for the Church and signs of the "new springtime".

Chapter Five

The Church's reflection on the priesthood

There is little doubt that the priesthood went through a serious crisis in identity during the 1970s and beyond. There were large-scale defections from the priesthood. Many priests became unclear about their identity. Many were disheartened and uncertain about their future. The traditional understanding of the role of the priest was being questioned and priestly celibacy was under serious discussion. Seminaries which were full only a decade before began to empty. Moreover there was a crisis in seminary education as many of the old and trusted ways were discarded in search of a new mode of formation. As we know only too well now, some seminaries slipped into serious moral and spiritual decay. These were dark times for priests and the priesthood.

The Church responded by seeking to rebuild an understanding of the nature of the priestly life and ministry. It reflected on the spiritual and theological understanding of the priesthood, seeking to reaffirm what is essential to priesthood and to address the particular challenges that priests faced.

Documents on the nature of the priesthood

A number of documents related to the priesthood were produced, particularly in the 1990s. In fact there is in evidence a refinement not only in the theology of the priesthood, but a clarification of the nature of priestly life and ministry in the contemporary Church and world. A succession of statements and documents reveal a serious and sustained effort to bring greater definition to the nature of priestly life in our time.

The magisterial foundations of this thought are to be found in the document on the priesthood from the Vatican Council, *Presbyterorum Ordinis,* and the teaching and vision of priesthood contained in the Constitution on the Church, *Lumen Gentium.* These magisterial efforts are supported by later works like the *Catechism of the Catholic Church* (1997) and the revised the *Code of Canon Law* (1983).

Pope John Paul had a particular affection for priests, and he clearly wanted to reaffirm priests in their identity and role in the Church. This was revealed in a practice which he commenced in 1979 of offering a "Letter to Priests" each Holy Thursday, something he continued throughout his pontificate. No doubt his effort here was fuelled by his awareness of the large numbers of priests struggling in their ministry. He sought to confirm and encourage priests during this difficult time.

He devoted a series of seventeen Wednesday audience talks during 1993 to pastoral reflections on priestly ministry. After an initial consideration of the nature of the priesthood, the Pope explored priestly spirituality and the pastoral life of priests. These reveal his own deep pastoral sense and were no doubt the fruit of his own experience of priestly ministry. They reveal Pope John Paul II's love for the priesthood in its expression in parish ministry.

Pastores dabo vobis

The 1990 synod of bishops addressed the issue of formation of priests. The resulting Apostolic Exhortation, *Pastores dabo vobis* (1992) not only provided a clear programme to be implemented in seminaries, but also provided a realistic contemporary understanding of the challenges facing priests. It sought to more adequately prepare men to be priests for the Church and world of this time. The document began with a lengthy analysis on the current situation of the Church in society. In considering the question of vocations to the priesthood it looked into the circumstances of contemporary youth culture.

In the face of a significant decline in vocations the document reaffirmed that the priesthood was essential to the Church:

> Without priests the Church would not be able to live that fundamental obedience which is at the very heart of her existence and her mission in history, an obedience in response to the command of Christ: "Go therefore and make disciples of all nations" (Mt 28:19) and "Do this in remembrance of me" (Lk 22:19; cf. 1 Cor 11:24), i.e., an obedience to the command to announce the Gospel and to renew daily the sacrifice of the giving of his body and the shedding of his blood for the life of the world.[27]

The document provides a serious exploration of the nature of the priesthood before devoting itself to the question of the formation of seminarians. This reveals that the times required a careful examination of what sort of priest is needed. In this we notice an effort to consider the particular expression that the priesthood needs to take in order to be able to effectively engage with the people. It is understood that times have changed and new challenges to priestly ministry need to be faced.

The document approaches the issue of formation of

---

27 *Pastores dabo vobis*, n. 1.

seminarians in a fresh way. It identifies the "four pillars" on which a priestly vocation can be built: the human, the spiritual, the pastoral and the academic. What is notable in the identification of these four essential elements of priestly formation is that the human formation of the priest is seen as the foundation upon which the other elements are to be developed. While the importance of the spiritual formation is clearly understood, the pastoral formation is given a stronger emphasis in this document. Placing the academic formation at the end of this sequence reveals a recognition that it is the formation of the character of the seminarian that must underpin the focus on academic formation.

The very title for the document, taking the words of the Lord given to the prophet Jeremiah, "I will give you shepherds after my own heart" (Jer 3:15), points to the aim of the document. The Church seeks to produce priests who are profoundly engaged with the heart of God. This focus is to be the wellspring of their ministry. It also testifies to a focus on the pastoral dimension of the ministry of the priest. The priest is to be a shepherd, willing to lay down his life in pastoral service of the people. The document sets forth a renewed direction for the adequate preparation of men to take on the challenge of being "priests for the new millennium".

Gift and Mystery

Pope John Paul's own love for the priesthood was expressed in his book, *Gift and Mystery* (1996), written to commemorate his anniversary of fifty years a priest. It is a deeply personal reflection that shows forth his great love for his own priesthood and his affection for priests. The Pope has no doubt as to the role that priests can play in society today:

> If we take a close look at what contemporary men and
> women expect from priests, we will see that, in the end,
> they have but one great expectation: they are thirsting

for Christ.[28]

He encourages priests to live "in the today of Christ"[29]: "If we immerse our human and priestly "today" in the "today" of Jesus Christ, there is no danger that we will become out-of-date, belonging to "yesterday".[30] He ended his book of personal reflection in an appeal to "my bothers in the priesthood" and particularly addressed those "experiencing a time of difficulty or even a crisis" in their vocation, stating:

> I would like my personal testimony – the testimony of a priest and the Bishop of Rome, who is celebrating the Golden Jubilee of his ordination – to be for you a help and an invitation to faithfulness. I have written these words thinking of each one of you and I embrace each one of you in my prayers.[31]

He invited priests who were likewise celebrating their golden anniversary to join him in a Mass and sixteen hundred priests participated in a concelebrated Mass.

Congregation for the Clergy

The Congregation for the Clergy has produced a number of significant documents in recent years. At the Synod in 1990 the bishops requested a document on priestly life and ministry to be prepared as an assistance to priests. As a result *The Directory on the ministry and life of Priests* (1994) was produced. It was directed to priests and provided a very useful guide to living priestly life. Identifying its purpose it stated:

> It is hoped that this Directory be a help for every priest in deepening his identity and in growing in

---

28 *Gift and Mystery*, p. 85.
29 Ibid., p. 84.
30 Ibid., p. 84.
31 Ibid., p. 97.

his spirituality; an encouragement in the ministry
and permanent formation — for which each one is
primarily responsible — and a point of reference for
a rich and authentic apostolate for the good of the
Church and of the entire world.[32]

This directory sought to move beyond a theological reflection
on the priesthood and consider a wide range of aspects of the life
of priests. It spoke to issues of the qualities needed for a priest as
well as priests receiving effective support from one another. The
directory was clearly aware of the challenges that priests faced,
and it sought to offer advice and guidance to them. It revealed
a clear sympathy with what priests were experiencing and it
wanted to affirm particularly that priests were part of a priestly
brotherhood.

Other documents followed, like the Interdicasterial Instruction,
Ecclesiae de mysterio (1997), an "instruction on certain questions
regarding the collaboration of the Non-Ordained faithful in the
sacred ministry of Priests". This instruction tackled particular
issues arising from the increased involvement of lay people in the
pastoral activities of the parish and offered a number of quite
specific clarifications as to the limits of lay participation to ensure
that the distinctive role of the priest was not compromised.

The two "Circular Letters", *The Priest and the Third Christian
Millennium, Teacher of the Word, Minister of the Sacraments and Leader
of the Community* (1999) and *The Priest, pastor and leader of the
parish community* (2002) contributed further reflection on priestly
ministry.

The first letter gave attention to the challenges brought on
by secularisation and encouraged priests to embrace the "New
Evangelisation". This letter, written on the eve of the new
millennium, sought to identify the particular challenges priests

---

32 Introduction by Cardinal Sanchez, Prefect of the Congregation for the Clergy.

face at this moment in history. It highlighted the role of the priest in being a minister of the Word of God. It spoke to priests about the need to respond effectively to the increasing inroads that secularism is having on the faith of the people:

> It is, therefore, necessary to assist both secular and religious priests in assuming the "important pastoral responsibility of new evangelisation" and, in the light of this commitment, to rediscover the divine call to serve that portion of God's people entrusted to them as teachers of the Word, ministers of the Sacraments and pastors of the flock.[33]

This document recognises that times have changed and that the traditional mode of operation of the priest in the parish community is no longer as effective as it has been in the past. There is a new reality that must be faced. Quoting the words of the Pope during an allocution to a Symposium of European Bishops,[34] it says, "heralds of the Gospel are needed who are expert in humanity, profoundly knowing the heart of contemporary man, who share his joys and hopes, his fears and sorrows, and, at the same time, who are contemplatives in love with God". This document highlights the process of de-Christianisation which any priest in a First World country would be able to recognise, and proposes a new way of approaching priestly ministry. The priest in the parish needs to take initiative in preaching and teaching in such a way that he is able to assist people in discovering afresh the Christian faith. Priests are called upon to find ways in which they can evangelise. It is a timely and challenging document for priests working among the people in ordinary parishes.

The second document focused attention on the role of the priest in the parish environment. It is a strong affirmation of the

---

33 Ibid.
34 *Insegnamenti di Giovanni Paolo II*, VIII, 2 (11 November 1985), pp. 918-919.

vital role of the parish in the life of the Church. It explores in detail the office of parish priest. In the introduction this theme is announced:

> This "Instruction" has the underlying purpose of directing particular affection towards those priests who carry out their precious office as Parish Priests and who, though beset by many challenges, are always in the midst of their people.[35]

While re-enforcing the key role of the priest in the parish, the document also explores the issues surrounding the role of collaboration with lay people, particularly in the light of the lack of sufficient priests to meet pastoral needs.

There is a focus on reinvigorating parishes and there is talk about basic programmes that can strengthen and renew parish life. Entering the new millennium the document speaks of "an exciting work of pastoral revitalisation".[36]

Novo Millennio Ineunte

Finally *Novo Millennio Ineunte*, written by Pope John Paul II as the Church entered the new millennium, provides a pastoral vision for the Church, something of particular relevance for priests. It is a forward looking document and focuses on pastoral issues.

In looking to the future of the Church in the new millennium the Pope says that it is not a matter of inventing a new programme, but rather he proposes that the Church concentrate on its essential areas of ministry – and then he goes on to list "certain pastoral priorities". These are not new, but he wants all, priests and lay people, to "start afresh from Christ". The Pope proposes that local Churches look to ways to achieve a pastoral revitalisation.

---

35 Introduction by Cardinal Sanchez, Prefect of the Congregation for the Clergy.
36 *The Priest, Pastor and leader of the Parish Community*, n. 27.

The Pope's proposals are the priorities in the heart of any priest, particularly priests working in parishes. His proposals for what is needed for the future of the Church are a clear affirmation of priestly life and ministry. He lists a number of proposals and it is worth noting them in a little detail.

He begins by referring back to Vatican II's "universal call to holiness" found in *Lumen Gentium*, n. 5. The Council reminded us that all the baptised are called to holiness. Pope John Paul says that there can be no programme for holiness. Holiness is something sought for its own sake. The work of a priest is not just the round of parish activities, but is inspired by and seeks to promote holiness of life. A key to this, the Pope argues, is developing the "art of prayer" – as he describes it, the "opening of the heart to the love of God". The Pope is aware that there is an emerging interest in prayer and he encourages priests to be instruments of fostering prayer in the lives of the people.

The centrality of the Sunday celebration of the Eucharist is highlighted as vital to Catholic life. The Pope mentions his document *Dies domini* (1998) and questions: Can we reverse the trends in our culture so that the celebration of the Eucharist becomes once again the heart of Sunday?

The spiritual dimension of the life and ministry of the Church is never far from his thoughts. The Pope raises the question of the primacy of Grace, and quotes John 15:5: "without Christ we can do nothing". Like the miraculous draft of fish told in the Gospel of St Luke, chapter 5, the Pope reminds us that it is the action of God and not of us that is important in pastoral ministry. Then the Pope goes on to speak of the listening to and proclaiming of the Word of God, harkening back to the thrust of the Second Vatican Council to make the Word of God the living inspiration of the pastoral action of the Church. In this context he refers to his conviction of the importance of the New Evangelisation for the Church of our time.

The letter is replete with a confident approach to the future. He shows no weariness or lack of hope about the future:

> Now we must look ahead, we must "put out into the deep", trusting in Christ's words: *Duc in altum!* What we have done this year cannot justify a sense of complacency, and still less should it lead us to relax our commitment. On the contrary, the experiences we have had should *inspire in us new energy*, and impel us to invest in concrete initiatives the enthusiasm which we have felt. Jesus himself warns us: "No one who puts his hand to the plough and looks back is fit for the kingdom of God" (Lk 9:62). In the cause of the Kingdom there is no time for looking back, even less for settling into laziness. Much awaits us, and for this reason we must set about drawing up an effective post-Jubilee pastoral plan.[37]

The Pope, even though in the twilight of his pontificate, could still look forward with great hope and expectation to the future, and he proposes that the Church, particularly at the local level, devise a pastoral plan to map out a future direction.

---

37 *Novo Millennio Ineunte*, n. 15.

Chapter Six

Identity of the priest

How do we understand who a priest is?

This question needs to be asked today because the question of the priesthood has been widely discussed. Prompted particularly by the decline in vocations in countries like Australia and the aging of priests, many have begun to raise questions about what the priesthood is. There is a wide ranging debate about the question as to whether the time has come for a change in the approach to priestly ministry.

Voices have been raised challenging the traditional understanding of the priesthood, urging a serious rethink. A number of issues have emerged in recent years that have created some confusion about the distinctive identity of the priest. Not only are some lay people questioning things, but priests themselves can go through soul searching and uncertainty. No priest can escape the questions being put to him. Has the time come to refashion the nature of the priesthood?

Contemporary questions about the priesthood

The need for a celibate clergy has been a constant subject of discussion. It is regularly raised in the media and many Mass-going Catholics state that they are open to a married priesthood. Many believe that the answer to the decline in vocations to the priesthood will be found in allowing priests to marry. There is discussion about the ordaining of "viri probati".[38] There are those who call for the opportunity for those priests who have left the ministry and married to be able to resume their priestly duties, and indeed there are many of them who would want to do this.

There continues to be a steady cry for the priesthood to be made open to women. Despite the definitive statement by Pope John Paul on this matter, there are still many who advocate women priests.[39] The fact that several Protestant denominations have chosen to have women ministers adds to the conviction of some that the Catholic Church is out of touch with the times. As most of the churches that are operative in Australia have now accepted women as ministers, and even bishops, the Catholic Church is more and more isolated in its position.

Another issue affecting the identity of priests is that of an uncertainty about the lines of delineation between the role of priests and the role of the lay person. Lay people are exercising roles in the liturgy, they are becoming "chaplains" in hospitals and prisons, and are in some cases being asked to have pastoral leadership in parish communities where there is no resident priest. There is emerging a certain "clericalisation" of the laity that blurs the distinction of what is specifically priestly ministry and what is proper to the laity.

---

38 "Viri probati" is a term that refers to men who are married at the time they are ordained a deacon, priest or bishop. Some people are proposing that this custom, found in the early Church, should be reintroduced to allow married men to be ordained as priests.

39 In *Ordinatio Sacerdotalis* (1994) the Pope stated, "Wherefore, in order that all doubt may be removed regarding a matter of great importance, a matter which pertains to the Church's divine constitution itself, in virtue of my ministry of confirming the brethren (see Lk 22:32) I declare that the Church has no authority whatsoever to confer priestly ordination on women and that this judgment is to be definitively held by all the Church's faithful".

Other issues concerning the identity of priests revolve around the actual role of the priest in the parish – is he the community leader, the president of the assembly, or is he more than this? There has been a strong focus on the pastoral role of the priest in its human dimension, but this can be at a cost of recognising his essential sacred ministry.

In the face of these and other issues it is important to develop a sound understanding of the identity of the priest.

The Common and Ministerial Priesthood

The Second Vatican Council spoke of the common priesthood of the faithful. It taught that the baptismal or *common priesthood* of Christians, which is a genuine participation in the priesthood of Christ, is an essential property of the New People of God.[40] We have witnessed a great growth in the participation of lay people at all levels of the work of the Church. At the local parish level we have witnessed an extraordinary growth of lay participation over the past twenty years. Within the liturgy Acolytes, Readers, Extraordinary Ministers of Holy Communion are now commonplace in most parishes. Lay people assist in preparation of children for the sacraments, and in some places lay people assist couples preparing for marriage and parents preparing for Baptism. Parishioners are involved in a wide range of parish groups. Parish councils and finance committees are a stable part of parish structures.

There is also a growing bureaucracy in areas like education, social welfare and health care composed of lay people. This has been one of the most significant developments in the Church in our time, and it is good. From a time when the work of the Church was in the hands of priests and religious, we now have the situation that large sectors of the Church are essentially run by lay people. This is in fact a realisation of the baptismal priesthood of each Catholic.

---

40 See *Lumen gentium*, nn. 10-11; *Presbyterorum Ordinis*, n. 2.

This extraordinary growth of active lay participation in the ministry of the Church raises the question of where a line can be drawn between those aspects of the Church in which lay people can contribute and those aspects of the Church that are rightfully reserved for priests. This is not an idle question as parish communities, particularly in rural situations, lack an effective presence of a priest. The issue of Sunday Communion Services conducted, in the absence of a priest, by lay people raises some important questions. Another question inevitably comes to be asked: could not a suitable lay person be appointed (or employed) to pastorally administer the parish?

The question of the distinctive nature of the priesthood is now of vital importance. Is the priesthood simply a role, a function carried out, or is it more than this?

The Metaphysics of Priesthood

One difficulty we face in dealing with this question is that of foundational theological thinking about the priesthood. The Church's theology is grounded in philosophy. Seminarians study philosophy for two years before they tackle four years of theology. Philosophy provides the intellectual tools to be able to develop theology. A key philosophical area is that of metaphysics. The Church's whole sacramental understanding is based on metaphysics.

When a person is baptised they are changed in who they are. They are now a Christian, a Catholic. They receive the Holy Spirit which makes them sons or daughters of God. Their identity is changed. When a couple are married they are changed. They become husband and wife. The two become one. They can no longer see themselves and their identity in the same way as they did before they were married. An ontological change, a change in being, has taken place.

Thus it is with the priesthood. A man once ordained is ontologically changed. He is a priest. Something mysterious happens. It is an action of grace, and something quite real.

The priesthood then is not just the deputing of an individual to take on a particular role. It is more than a function: it is a radical re-orienting of the whole reality of the person. He is changed at the level of his being. The text from Psalm 110 is often used in relation to Ordination to the priesthood: "you are a priest forever, according to the order of Melchizedek" (Ps110:4). The priesthood is a matter of a change in being that is permanent and irreversible. Thus the priesthood cannot be understood as something temporary and functional.

The priest is invested with the character and grace of the Sacrament of Orders by virtue of a call from God ratified by the Church in the Sacrament. The ministerial priesthood and the common priesthood of the faithful are different from each other not just in degree but in essence, the Church teaches.[41]

We can speak of a man receiving a "priestly character" through ordination. Ordination is not just the power to exercise the priestly office in the Church; it is such a transformation of the person that a distinctly priestly character can be identified in him. He is shaped and moulded into a priest. He takes on the priesthood which is found in Christ.

In persona Christi

There is only one priesthood, that of Christ. As the *Letter to the Hebrews* teaches, Christ has "an unchangeable priesthood" (Heb7:24), which endures forever. The *Letter to the Hebrews* runs the argument that the Old Testament priesthood was an inherited priesthood exercised by the sons of Aaron offering sacrifices for sins over and over again. Christ, it argues, was designated priest

---

41 See *Lumen Gentium*, n. 10; *Presbyterorum Ordinis*, n. 2.

offering a perfect sacrifice by his death on the cross, and is now a priest forever. Psalm 110, "you are a priest forever", is quoted by the author of the Letter.

The priest acts *in persona Christi,* in the person of Christ the priest. This is a fundamental sense that a Catholic priest has, particularly at sacramental moments. The priest says when administering the sacraments, "I baptise; I absolve; This is my body…". It is clear at these moments that he is not acting on his own authority or exercising a personal power. He is acting in the name of Christ, *in persona Christi.* The "I" is not the individual priest but Christ. Thus, it is Christ who is acting in and through him. Simply, the ministry of the priest brings the saving power of Christ, won by his death on the cross, into people's lives.

The mind of Christ on this issue is very clear. From the inception of his public ministry Jesus quite deliberately sought out and called certain men to himself: "Come follow me and I will make you fishers of men" (Mk 1:17). In the Gospel of Mark, when the Lord sent out his disciples, he gave them authority not only to speak but to act in his name, drawing upon his power to heal and save: "He called the twelve and began to send them out two by two, and gave them authority over the unclean spirits". (Mk 6:7). They were to carry out <u>his</u> mission, act in <u>his</u> name, enabling <u>his</u> power to be manifested: "They cast out many demons, and anointed with oil many who were sick and cured them" (Mk 6:13).

This is the mystery, the power and the dignity of the priesthood. The priest acts in the name of Christ and with the power of Christ. Priests, though, are ordinary men, as the apostles were ordinary men. While their personal holiness is very important, and their particular gifts are important, in the end it is that God works through them, sometimes despite themselves.

To further strengthen the concept, Pope John Paul used the term *in persona Christi capitis,* in the person of "Christ the head". This was to highlight the fact that priestly ministry is directly linked to the role of Christ as head of his Body the Church. Pope John Paul II expressed this reality in these words:

> By sacramental consecration the priest is configured to Jesus Christ as head and shepherd of the Church, and he is endowed with a "spiritual power" which is a share in the authority with which Jesus Christ guides the Church through his Spirit.[42]

Christ is related to the Church as head and shepherd. St Paul teaches, "He is the head of the body, the Church" (Eph 1:22). Christ is the "Good Shepherd" who has laid down his life for the Church (Jn 10:15). Thus a priest not only engages the salvific power of Christ in sacramental moments, but he exercises a pastoral leadership in the name of Christ.

These reflections on the nature of the priesthood provide a basis for considering the issue of the admission of women to the priesthood. What is clear is that the priesthood by definition is profoundly linked to the person of Christ. It is more than just a role and function performed in the Church. It is more, too, than some form of power and authority exercised in its own right. The role of the priesthood is a participation in the priesthood of Christ, the Son of God, who was incarnate in the person of Jesus of Nazareth.

When the priest acts he acts as Christ. The fact that Christ was born male is not incidental to this. Thus, the Church teaches that the priesthood is only open to men.

Man of God

To continue to explore the nature of the priesthood it is good to ask: what is the essential task of the priest? Is he principally the leader of the parish community? Is his role a pastoral service to

---

42 *Pastores dabo vobis*, n. 21.

the community?

The classical text used to depict the specific nature of the priesthood is that in the *Letter to the Hebrews*, "Every high priest taken from among men is appointed for men in things pertaining to God, that he may offer both gifts and sacrifices for sins" (Heb 5:1). This text reminds us of the essential task of the priest. While there has been much emphasis placed on the pastoral role of the priest in the parish community, it is important to emphasise that his first and primary role is that of being an intermediary between God and people.

The Church would identify that his first role is to be a preacher of the Word of God (we will discuss this in some detail later). This task becomes all the more significant in the secular environment in which people live today. He is a man imbued with the Word of God who can then proclaim and preach it to the people. Thus a priest is one dedicated to sit before God in prayer and listen for the voice of God. He must be a man of prayer, devoted firstly to being the faithful disciple who daily attunes himself to the presence and mind of God.[43]

The priest is uniquely fulfilling his role of being an agent of the work of God when he celebrates the sacraments for the people. In each sacramental moment the priest, acting in the name of Christ, becomes the conduit of the grace of God. He is the conduit of mercy and forgiveness in the Sacrament of Penance. He becomes the conduit of the healing presence of the Lord for the dying in the Sacrament of Anointing. He is the conduit of the Holy Spirit changing bread and wine into the Body and Blood of Christ in the Mass.

The priest is simply the means by which the grace of God

---

43 See Is 50:5. The beautiful and moving "Servant Song" found in Isaiah presents this faithful servant of God who is attentive to the will and intentions of God, who "listens as a disciple", is prepared to be a "suffering servant", accepting abuse and ridicule and eventually physical suffering in the cause to which he has been called.

can enter and transform the lives of believers. The people sense this when they approach the priest and ask him to pray for their particular needs, or when they bring him an object to be blessed. They see him as a man of God.

The priest is only too aware of his own limitations and shortcomings. He knows that it is not him in himself that attracts the faith and hope of the people, but it is simply that he is a priest, consecrated to God through Holy Orders. It is not his holiness that is decisive in this, though growing in personal holiness is a particular responsibility of the priest, but it is the holiness of the Church expressed and realised in the priesthood. This is a humbling experience for the priest, but also the glory of the priesthood. Priests can comment that they often have felt humanly inadequate in particular situations, but the grace of the priesthood shone through and achieved what was beyond the capacity of the individual.

A spiritual father

People have traditionally addressed the priest as "father". A priest is seen as a spiritual father. He has renounced the possibility of generating children 'according to the flesh', to generate children "in the Spirit" (See Jn 1:13). The missions of evangelisation, catechesis, and the bestowing of sacraments are means by which a priest has a spiritual fruitfulness. St Paul understood this only too well. He said to the Corinthians, "For I became your father in Christ Jesus, through the Gospel" (1 Cor 4:15). He readily describes Timothy and Titus as "sons" (See 1 Tim1:2; Tt 1:3), and his letters to them reveal a depth of paternal care and advice.

Spiritual paternity is sometimes most evident in the relationship that a priest develops with young people, either at school or in youth movements. The young people readily look to him as having a fatherly role in their lives. Not only will they be open to receive his advice and guidance, but they seek to model themselves on aspects of his Christian character that they admire.

Nowhere is spiritual fatherhood more evident than in the confessional. People approach the priest with humility and openness, willing to expose their own fragility and struggles. They seek not only forgiveness but also encouragement and support. A priest often experiences his identity as father in moments of deep trusting intimacy in the confessional situation. In a way this is to be expected because the confessional is the practical realisation of the parable of the Prodigal Son. This wonderful parable told by St Luke (15:11-32) really focuses on the merciful heart of God the Father. The parable tells of the father who waits for the return of his errant son. He has never given up on him. He waits and when the son returns humbled and penitent, the father lavishes love upon him. Here is revealed the depth of the merciful heart of God the Father. A priest in the confessional becomes immediately engaged in this action of forgiveness. He becomes the words and gestures of God the Father receiving his child back into full and free relationship with him.

Pope John Paul captures this beautifully when he writes, no doubt reflecting his own experience of being a priest in the confessional:

> The priest is the witness and instrument of divine mercy! How important in his life is the ministry of the confessional! It is in the confessional that his *spiritual fatherhood* is realised in the fullest way. It is in the confessional that every priest becomes aware of the great miracles which divine mercy works in souls which receive the grace of conversion.[44]

Jesus reminded his disciples that there is only one Father and "we are all brothers" (Mt 23:9). A priest is a father in God. His

---

44 John Paul II, *Gift and Mystery*, London, 1996, p. 86.

fatherhood is derived from the one Father, but now bestowed "in the name of the Father". The fatherhood of the priest is grounded in the authentic fatherhood found in God Himself. A priest is in fact an icon of the fatherhood of God. A priest is an instrument whereby the fatherhood of God can be mediated to his children.

When Christ was baptised in the Jordan by John, he heard the words, "You are my Son, the Beloved, my favour rests on you" (Lk 3:22). For Jesus were there any more important words to be heard? He was affirmed in his identity and assured of an enduring love. Fatherhood means total self-giving love. A priest as father loves his people with a fully self-giving spirit. He is one whom the people know loves them and has a deep fatherly affection for them. He will not reject them, or impose any limits on his willingness to love them. That is why people will turn to the priest in moments of trial and darkness. They expect one who is available to embrace them and walk with them "in the valley of death" (see Ps 23:4).

The people look to the priest as a spiritual father. They see him as one who has laid down his life for them in the sense of the sacrifice of his life to the priesthood. Indeed, they prefer to relate to him as a father, rather than a mate. A priest, sure of who he is, will be content to be seen as a father, and will not want to water down the sacredness of the relationship.

Being a father is one of the singular sources of consolation for the priest. His life, his sacrifices, his dedication is to generate spiritual and moral life. This is no barren and futile existence! It is a means by which people are nourished and guided. The people want and need in the priest one whom they know as their father in God.

A man set apart

One of the most intriguing aspects of the priesthood is that it is the result not of a person's own desire to be a priest (though this can be a preliminary experience) but the awareness of a calling. "You did not choose me, no I chose you" (Jn 15:16) is something that many priests can relate to. The priesthood is an attraction, albeit mysterious. Men do feel drawn to it and see it as something they long to do, but the personal pull towards the priesthood is in the end not something from themselves. The prophet Jeremiah, a reluctant prophet, said in one place, "You seduced me, and I let myself be seduced" (Jer 20:7). Priests do find themselves "seduced" into the priesthood. There is some mysterious calling that draws them to it. It is something that does not diminish with time. It is not just a passing fad or superficial emotional attraction, it is a deep and abiding desire that seizes them at the deepest level of their being.

The Lord preached to the crowds and urged them to faith[45] but from the outset he called particular individuals, "Come follow me",[46] adding significantly "and I will make you fishers of men" (Mt 4:19). These chosen ones he would eventually name personally as his disciples (see Mt 10:2ff) and begin to train them to become "apostles", to carry on his work.

This same dynamic is operative today. All are urged to faith by the preaching of the Gospel, but some receive a call to become "fishers of men". They are asked to "leave everything" in order to devote themselves to the work of the Kingdom. They are men set apart for the purposes of God. This is expressed in the calling to the priesthood. The priesthood is a calling, a vocation. It is a gift from God given to those chosen by him.[47] At heart it is a mystery, a mystery of God's wondrous ways of choosing to act.

---

45 "Repent and believe for the Kingdom of God is close at hand" (Mt 4:17).
46 It is interesting to note that Matthew, immediately after stating that Jesus commenced his public preaching, speaks of Jesus walking by the Sea of Galilee and calling Peter, James and John. It would seem that from the very outset Jesus intended to draw particular individuals to himself whom he would prepare to be the ones to take up his mission.
47 "You did not choose me, no, I chose you" (Jn 15:16)

Pope John Paul in his reflections on his fifty years a priest spoke of his vocation as "Gift and Mystery".[48]

Celibate for the sake of the Kingdom

The advent of Christianity brought to the fore the notion of a celibate life for spiritual purposes. Judaism only had very limited appreciation of such a concept. Yet it figured strikingly among those closely linked to Jesus. The mother of Jesus, Mary, is honoured as "ever Virgin" by Christian tradition, acknowledging that she and St Joseph had a celibate relationship in marriage. Other key figures also lived celibate lives: St John the Baptist, St John the Evangelist, St Paul.[49] The Lord himself would teach that some among his followers would embrace celibacy "for the sake of the Kingdom" (Mt 19:12). St Paul would amplify this view in his letters, arguing that some would embrace celibacy in order to devote themselves "to the Lord's affairs". In his *First Letter to the Corinthians* he proposes that some will be prepared to accept celibacy in order to be unencumbered in giving their undivided attention to the Lord (See 1 Cor 7:32-35). He is obviously witnessing to an attitude among the Christians in Corinth.

In the first flush of religious zeal and enthusiasm the early Christians highly honoured those who chose a celibate path. Early "heroes" among the Christians were the virgins, especially the virgin martyrs whom we still hold in a prominent place in our liturgy.[50]

The embracing of celibacy for spiritual reasons was

---

48 His book, "Gift and Mystery" is a deeply personal and spiritual reflection on his life as a priest.

49 In his first letter to the Corinthians, in speaking about celibacy St Paul states that he is one who "by the Lord's mercy has stayed faithful" (1 Cor 7:25)

50 For example, St Agnes, St Cecilia, St Agatha, and others. The Roman Canon in the second list of saints mentions a number of virgin martyrs, witnessing to their special place among the saints.

"institutionalised" by the flourishing of monasticism in the third and fourth centuries, when hundreds, indeed thousands, of Christians experienced a call to pursue their spiritual life intensely in the deserts of Egypt, Palestine and Syria. The life of the individual hermit, or anchorite (St Antony of Egypt being the great exemplar), eventually gave way to communal, or coenobitic, life. It eventually devolved into the Benedictine monasticism that spread throughout Europe over the next thousand years.

Most of the apostles were presumably married; certainly St Peter was.[51] St Paul counselled that leaders within the Christian community should be proven men shown by their ability to manage their families well (See 1Tim 3:4). There is plenty of evidence that many early bishops were married men and sometimes their sons continued the work of their fathers.[52]

However, the Church came to see that celibacy was something appropriate for those who exercised the priestly office. Bishops were expected to refrain from intercourse with their wives prior to celebrating the Sunday liturgy.[53] In time, it was deemed appropriate that men on being called to be bishops would, with the approval of their wives, live in celibate marriage. The injunction of St Paul that an elder should not be the husband of more than one wife was seen as requiring bishops not to marry again should their wife die.

---

51 Reference is made in the New Testament to Peter's mother-in-law (Mt 8:14), though there is no specific reference to his wife.

52 A good example of this is St Gregory Nazianzus. He was son, one of three children, of Gregory, Bishop of Nazianzus (329-374), in the south-west of Cappadocia. He succeeded his father in the Episcopal see of Nazianzus.

53 There is the popular belief that celibacy was imposed on the clergy in the ninth century. However, there is clear evidence that celibacy was widely recognised and practised from the early centuries. There are a number of recent studies that present strong argument for this. A. Stickler, in the *Case for Clerical Celibacy, Its Historical Development and Theological Foundations* (Ignatius Press, San Francisco, 1995) argues the case very convincingly. Stefan Heid's *Celibacy in the Early Church* (Ignatius Press, San Francisco, 2000) is another well researched book.

Stefan Heid in his book *Celibacy in the Early Church* concludes his study of the situation in the Eastern Church in the fourth century by stating:

> We can accept as given an obligation of higher clerics to practice perpetual continence, whether they were virginal, widowed or married. For the island of Cyprus we have the testimony of Epiphanius of Salamis, for Palestine and Egypt that of Jerome, and for Syria and Asia Minor that of John Chrysostom, Theodore of Mopsuestia and Theodoret of Cyrrhus. Epiphanius states explicitly that continence constitutes a universally valid and binding norm.[54]

Increasingly the direction of the Church teaching was along the line of seeing the priestly ministry requiring a commitment to celibate life. This has become the practice of the Latin Church, while recognising the right of Eastern Churches to follow the practice of allowing married clergy (though they require bishops to be celibate).

The practice of celibacy is now strongly embedded in the living tradition of the Church and is not something that will be changed for pragmatic reasons in the face of a decline in vocations. In the end celibacy is not the hinge issue in regard to vocations to the priesthood. The critical issue is that of the general malaise in faith among many in the First World. Vocations continue to be strong in Africa, India, Vietnam, some Asian countries and in parts of the Pacific.

Celibacy is clearly a sacrifice that is asked by God of those called by God to the priesthood. It is a sacrifice along the same lines as the sacrifice involved in making a commitment of obedience to the bishop. It is an act of faith. It is done "for the sake of the Kingdom" and to enable the priest to be "devoted to the affairs of

---

54 Heid, p. 198.

the Lord" with singleness of heart.

Celibacy, while often difficult to understand by those outside the Church and indeed by some within the Church, is something greatly respected by the people. A Catholic knows and understands that the priest is singularly devoted to his role and ministry. He is called "Father" because he exercises a spiritual paternity. He is a spiritual father to all who seek his ministrations. People sense a man whose whole life is made available to God and the things of God, and who is among them as a servant. For these reasons Catholic people have enormous respect and love for their priests.

Some comments on the collaboration between priest and lay people

We noted earlier that increasingly parishioners have stepped up in collaboration with priests to enable parish communities to carry out their vital functions, not only in the areas of liturgy, but in important aspects of the priest's daily ministry, like taking Holy Communion to the sick in their homes, in nursing homes and hospitals. Catechists have enabled the teaching of the faith to be given to children attending State Schools. Parishes have seen a variety of "ministries" established to ensure that the parish is being pastorally active, for instance, bereavement teams, hospitality groups, RCIA teams. Some parishes can boast of literally hundreds of its parishioners contributing in one form or another to the work of parish. Parishes list dozens of organisations operating within the parish which nourish the Catholic life of the parish, like prayer groups, Scripture Study groups, social justice groups, ethnic groups, seniors, alongside the traditional organisations like St Vincent de Paul, Legion of Mary, Catholic Women's League and Knights of the Southern Cross.

There is no doubt that the level of lay participation in the Church has risen in the last decades. There is a sense abroad that a committed Catholic does not just come to Mass on Sunday but is involved in some way with the life and activities of the parish. This is a significant advance for the Church and a great source of strengthening the life of the Church.

As levels of participation have increased, a blurring of the respective roles of priest and lay person has emerged. For instance, as lay people have been taking Holy Communion to the sick, they have developed a familiarity with going up to the tabernacle to get the hosts. Sometimes it is simply for pragmatic reasons that lay people take on roles that are those of the priest. It can be in small things, like the Extraordinary Minister of Holy Communion going to the tabernacle to bring the Blessed Sacrament to the altar prior to the distribution of Holy Communion, or the altar server or Acolyte preparing the chalice by putting in the wine and water. These practices, which creep in as simple pragmatic ways of assisting the priest, draw lay people into roles and practices that are rightly those of the priest. We have a creeping "clericalisation of the laity".

In the instance when a parish community does not have the services of a priest on a Sunday, a Communion Service is held, led by a member of the parish. This practice has become commonplace in some, particularly rural, dioceses. It is an extension of the rite available to use for the sick: a penitential rite, a Scripture reading, a short admonition and then the Lord's Prayer and the reception of Holy Communion.[55]

---

55 The Sacred Congregation for Divine Worship in 1973 issued a Decree concerning *Holy Communion and Worship of the Eucharist Outside Mass*. The Introduction to the Rite acknowledged that while Sacramental Communion is intended to be received during Mass, circumstances may arise where people request receiving Holy Communion outside of Mass. The Introduction to the Rite comments that "Priests are not to refuse to give Communion to the faithful who ask for it even outside Mass" (n. 14). A *Rite of Distributing Holy Communion outside Mass* proposes a form including a Celebration of the Word. It is this proposal that has been seen as meeting the need of communities who are not able to have a Sunday Mass. The Rite, in offering this option, did not envisage this becoming a standard practice in parish communities.

It has come to be seen as the most suitable replacement for the actual celebration of Mass, but as time goes on the widespread practice raises some important questions. Communities can feel that they can manage quite well by themselves. Certainly the priest must still consecrate the hosts, but the actual liturgical action seems to be quite adequately met by a lay person, or a religious. Sometimes indeed they can feel that they are managing better without the priest! The Communion Service seems to meet the spiritual needs – the Scriptures are read and Holy Communion is received! The Rite of Distributing Holy Communion outside Mass was intended as an extraordinary option, it was not intended to become the rule, and be seen as an alternative to the celebration of Mass.

At a Communion Service the Mass is not celebrated. The liturgical action is not carried out. Strictly speaking this community did not do what the Lord commanded: "Do this in memory of me". The Eucharistic Prayer, the solemn prayer of praise and worship was not said and the Last Supper was not commemorated by the words and action of a priest representing Christ. The community gathered for receiving Holy Communion, but not for the commemoration and actualisation of the mystery of salvation, which only the Mass can effect.

Pope John Paul made an interesting comment in an address to the Congregation for the Clergy: "Without the presence of Christ, represented by the priest, who is the spiritual leader of the community, this would not fully be an ecclesial communion".[56] In other words, a parish community without a priest is not fully being what the Church is meant to be. Parish communities cannot see themselves as able to be true communities without the priest and the celebration of the Mass.

It may be time to reconsider the advisability of replacing Mass

---

56 Address to the Plenary Meeting of the Congregation for the Clergy (23 November 2001).

with Communion Services. There could be a more appropriate approach to take in having the community come together for the celebration of the Liturgy of the Hours which is the other key liturgical action of the Church, offering a "sacrifice of praise". A yearning for the celebration of the Mass through the ministry of a priest can actually heighten an appreciation of the immense value of the Mass in Catholic life and become a further stimulus to beg God for an increase in vocations to the priesthood.

In 1997 the Congregation for the Clergy, the Pontifical Council for the Laity and the Congregation for the Doctrine of the Faith combined to produce the document, *On certain questions regarding the collaboration of the non-ordained faithful in the sacred ministry of the priest.*[57] This document identified key areas where clarification about the respective roles of lay persons and priests was needed.

The document begins by raising the question of the use of appropriate terminology. The question of the use of the word "ministry" in relation to roles performed by lay people was questioned. The document recommends that lay people do not see themselves as "ministers", but rather occupying a ministerial role for a particular time and purpose. It goes on to say that the words, "pastor" and "chaplain" should only be used to designate a role exercised by a member of the clergy.

The document addresses the question of lay people preaching in the Church and then specifically addresses the question of the preaching of the homily. A lay person can be called upon to preach or teach in the Church, but there must be delegation from the bishop. "Preaching in churches or oratories by the non-ordained faithful can be permitted only as a *supply* for sacred ministers or for those particular reasons foreseen by the universal law of the Church or by Conferences of Bishops. It cannot, however, be regarded as an ordinary occurrence nor as an authentic promotion

---

57 Promulgated on August 15, 1997.

of the laity"[58]. The homily at Mass is to be the domain of the clergy, and even seminarians are not permitted to preach.[59]

Quoting Canon 517, the document emphasises that the parish priest alone can direct, coordinate, moderate or govern the parish. It stresses that parish councils are consultative and should be presided over by the parish priest. They cannot make decisions apart from nor contrary to him.

In the liturgy the lay people may not say words reserved for the priest or in any way "quasi preside" at Eucharistic celebrations. Where no priest is available the document stipulates that a lay person must be deputed by the bishop: "This mandate should contain specific instructions with regard to the term of applicability, the place and conditions in which it is operative, as well as indicate the priest responsible for overseeing these celebrations".[60]

In relation to the role of lay persons assisting in the distribution of Holy Communion, the document emphasises that such a role should be seen as "supplementary and extraordinary".[61]

The document addresses the roles of lay persons in the "apostolate to the sick", "assistance at Marriages", "Ministers of Baptism" and "leading the celebration at funerals". In all these cases care is urged to ensure that a lay person steps into a role only when there is absolute necessity. Throughout this document the underlying theme is that the ordinary minister in the Church's pastoral and liturgical life is the priest and all must be done to ensure that this understanding is not lost.

---

58 *On certain questions regarding the collaboration of the non-ordained faithful in the sacred ministry of the priest*, Article 2, n. 4.

59 See Canon 766.

60 *On certain questions regarding the collaboration of the non-ordained faithful in the sacred ministry of the priest*, Article 7, n. 1.

61 Ibid., Article 8, n. 2.

A note on Holy Orders

Our attention in this book is on the life and ministry of priests. It is important to situate our considerations within the broader context of the Church's understanding of Holy Orders. The Church speaks of the "three degrees" of Holy Orders: episcopate, presbyterate, and deaconate.[62] A person is ordained into one of these degrees by the sacramental act of the laying on of hands accompanied by a consecratory prayer. A person is "ordained" and by virtue of this can exercise "sacred power".[63] Two of these degrees of Holy Orders are a ministerial participation in the priesthood of Christ: the episcopate and the presbyterate. Deacons are ordained for a ministry of service.

Bishops have the fullness of the sacrament of Holy Orders and are successors of the Apostles. Each bishop enjoys an unbroken succession traced back to apostolic times. A bishop is entrusted with the care of a particular church, a diocese, and in a collegial spirit with his brother bishops is to have "solicitude for all the churches".[64]

The Catechism of the Catholic Church describes priests as "co-workers of the bishops".[65] Quoting the teaching of the Second Vatican Council the Catechism teaches,

> The function of the bishops' ministry was handed over in a subordinate degree to priests so that they might be appointed in the order of the priesthood and be co-workers of the Episcopal order for the proper fulfilment of the apostolic mission that had been entrusted to it by Christ.[66]

---

62 *Catechism of the Catholic Church*, 1536.
63 See *Catechism of the Catholic Church*, 1538.
64 See 2 Cor 11:28.
65 *Catechism of the Catholic Church*, 1562.
66 *Presbyterorum Ordinis*, n. 2; *Catechism of the Catholic Church*, 1562.

Thus, for the priest, the exercise of his ministry is always related to the bishop. This gives rise to the strong bonds that exist between priest and bishop. These bonds are at once based on a dependence and at the same time seen as fraternal. Priests can only exercise their powers and their ministry in relation to a bishop, but at the same time they share with the bishop a sacerdotal dignity.

Deacons receive the imposition of hands not for priesthood but for ministry. The early Church witnesses to the high regard in which deacons were held: Do all "in union with your most worthy bishop, with the precious spiritual crown of your presbytery and with your deacons according to God".[67] In fact we can notice that deacons are often referred to in relation to the bishop.[68] Deacons had a key role in the Church as helpers of bishops. St Sixtus, bishop of Rome, was martyred with four of his deacons; a fifth deacon, Lawrence, was martyred some days later because the Roman authorities thought he had care of the finances of the diocese. It is clear that the bishop had a group of deacons who assisted him, carrying out more administrative and organisational tasks.

The Second Vatican Council, rightly, sought to restore the ancient custom of the presence of permanent deacons in the diocese. The Church had preserved the diaconate as a stage towards priestly ordination, not seeing it as an order in its own right. One could argue that a diocese is not really complete without the presence of a good number of deacons. Deacons have the role of assisting, not only liturgically but also practically, in the life of the diocese, especially around the bishop. The development of the diaconate remains a "work in progress" for the Church in Australia.

---

67 St Ignatius of Antioch, *Magn.*13.1.
68 "Since a long time the Scriptures spoke of bishops and deacons". St Clement, bishop of Rome. Cor 42:5.

The indispensable place of priests

While recognising the appropriate roles for bishops and deacons, it is nonetheless true that priests are indispensable to the life of the Church in its daily life. The work of the Church, particularly in its preaching and sacramental task, is carried out in parishes through the ministry of priests. The Church is dependent on them, not only for their sacramental ministry, but also to be the face of Christ the Good Shepherd in the midst of his flock.

That face is a human face, unique to each priest. We will now consider the humanity of the priesthood.

Chapter Seven

The humanity of the priest

The priesthood is incarnated in the human character of the priest. St John declares in the opening chapter of his Gospel: "The Word became flesh" (Jn 1:14). So the priesthood "becomes flesh" in a particular individual. The human element of the priesthood is both a limit to and the glory of the priesthood. Priests are ordinary human beings with the limitations and foibles that mark the life of each man. Yet the priesthood inspires and transforms frail and imperfect individuals. The highest of ideals for human character and the unfolding of a human life can be realised through the priesthood. The history of the priesthood in the Church reveals men rising to become extraordinary individuals and living heroic lives of dedication and service. Priests have developed the noblest of human qualities. They have been great leaders, compassionate fathers, self-sacrificing servants of the people and dedicated witnesses to the Gospel ideals. They have been able to reach out to and be instruments of the grace of God to people of extraordinarily diverse situations and needs.

The Instruction, *The Priest, Pastor and Leader of the Parish Community*,[69] expresses this great tradition of priestly achievement

---

69 Issued by the Congregation for the Clergy, 4 August 2002.

in these words:

> The Church's history is redolent with splendid models
> of truly radical pastoral self-sacrifice. These include
> a great number of holy priests who have reached
> sanctity through generous and indefatigable dedication
> to the care of souls, commitment to asceticism and a
> profound spiritual life, among them the Curé of Ars,
> patron of parish priests. These pastors, consumed by
> the love of Christ and its attendant pastoral charity, are
> a lived expression of the Gospel.[70]

Human qualities are a bridge

The human realisation of the priesthood is described as a "bridge"
in *Pastores dabo vobis*.[71] This document on the formation of priests
gives attention first to the question of the human formation of
seminarians. This is seen as the "necessary foundation"[72] to all
formation for the priesthood. A priest by the very nature of his life
is involved with people. He engages with people on a daily basis.
His character, his human traits, are the vital bridge, the conduit for
his ministry.

> In order that his ministry may be humanly as credible
> and acceptable as possible, it is important that the
> priest should mould his human personality in such a
> way that it becomes a bridge and not an obstacle for
> others in their meeting with Jesus Christ the Redeemer
> of humanity.[73]

Thus the human qualities of the priest are of great importance if he

---

70 Ibid., n. 11.
71 *Pastores dabo vobis*, n. 43.
72 Ibid.
73 Ibid.

is to be able to be effective as a priest. The document lists some of the qualities a seminarian should develop if he is to be a successful priest. They can be a simple checklist for a priest. The document says that a priest must be balanced, strong and free, capable of bearing the weight of pastoral responsibilities. A priest must love the truth, be loyal, respect every person, have a sense of justice, be true to his word, be genuinely compassionate, be a man of integrity and, especially, be balanced in judgment and behaviour.[74] A priest must be able to relate to people in all walks of life. *Pastores dabo vobis* speaks of the priest as a "man of communion", capable of an openness and responsiveness to people, "affable, hospitable, sincere in his words and heart, prudent and discreet, generous and ready to serve, capable of opening himself to clear and brotherly relationships and of encouraging the same in others, and quick to understand, forgive and console."[75]

Walking the path of virtue

A way to approach this question of the fostering of the human qualities of the priest is to look again at the Church's teaching on virtue. In an age which speaks about "values" and "ethos" which can tend towards the vague, the classical Catholic teaching on virtue is worth examining. Virtue is described as "an habitual and firm disposition to do good."[76] Virtues are grounded in a prevailing disposition of the person to pursue the morally good life. They involve a firm decision grounded in intellect and will to develop a self mastery which enables the practice of good to become habitual.

Within the Christian tradition, virtue is a work of the person aided by divine grace. Growth in virtue is not solely the result of

---

74 Ibid.
75 Ibid.
76 *Catechism of The Catholic Church*, 1803.

willpower and determination. The Christian life is the life of grace. It is the outpouring of the Holy Spirit that produces good fruit in the life of each Christian.[77] In classical works on the spiritual life the pursuit of virtue is the necessary foundation to growth in interior prayer.[78] Indeed, the Christian life is not just moral right living through the avoidance of sin, but has a specific positive thrust in the effort to foster the life of virtue.

Growth in virtue is in fact growth in our humanity, modelling the image of God in which we were created (Gen 1:27). It is the way to become truly and fully human. The path of virtue is the process of becoming what God intended us to be. The true nature of our humanity is disfigured by sin. The virtues restore what sin has damaged. Christ, God made man, is the model of true and full humanity. Growth in virtue is growth in Christ-likeness.

Following the insights of ancient Greek philosophy and attested in the Wisdom literature of the Old Testament, the various human virtues have been clustered around the four "cardinal virtues": prudence, justice, fortitude and temperance.[79] This classical structuring of the virtues is but one way of approaching and listing the virtues. Traditional Catholic teaching on the virtues distinguishes those that are the supernatural virtues – Faith, Hope and Love – and the human or moral virtues as given above. They can be distinguished by reason of their source – nature or grace –

---

77 See Gal 5:22-23: "The fruit of the Spirit is love, joy, peace, patience, kindness, generosity, faithfulness, gentleness, and self control".
78 The very well known classic spiritual work, *Imitation of Christ*, has as key spiritual concepts: *Conversio*: embracing the Christian life; *Resolutio*: a personal resolution to walk this path; *Exercitium*: spiritual training, the practice of the virtues; *Profectus virtutum*: progress in the virtues; Caritas: the goal of love; *Humilitas*: the need to be humble; *Obedientia*: the breaking of one's own will; *Cor*: a focus on the heart, rather than the mind; *Affectus*: cultivation of the right affections, i.e., purity of heart.
79 See Wis 8:7. The Cardinal Virtues were spoken of by the Hellenistic Jew, Philo of Alexandria, and referred to by the early Fathers of the Church, e.g., Clement of Alexandria, Origen, the Cappadocians, Ambrose, Jerome, Augustine, Gregory the Great. See Benedict Ashley OP, *Living the Truth in Love*, 1996

and their object – God or neighbour.

The virtues can be viewed as Christian in that they flow from Christian teaching or they can be viewed as human in that they achieve a wholeness and perfecting of human character.

What are the key virtues that should be fostered in the life of a priest?

Pastoral Charity

The virtues most appropriate for a priest would be those that contribute to his role as pastor of the Christian community and can be clustered around the governing virtue of pastoral charity. The priest is called to be a pastor, a shepherd of the people entrusted to his care. By virtue of the Sacrament of Orders, being "configured to Christ", the life of the priest is "marked, moulded and characterised by the way of thinking and acting proper to Jesus Christ, head and shepherd of the Church, and which are summed up in his pastoral charity".[80] The priest naturally takes Christ as his reference point when considering the way in which he conducts his pastoral ministry. The quality of the relationships that Christ had with people inspires the priest.

The human character of Christ can be a rich source of reflection on the nature of pastoral charity. The Lord reveals in his public ministry a great capacity to accept people of all different backgrounds and levels of spiritual and moral life. One can think of the conversation with the woman at the well (see Jn 4:5-30), the engaging of Zaccheus (see Lk 19:1-10), the widow at Nain (see Lk 7:11-17), his choice of Matthew the tax collector as one of his disciples (see Mk 2:13-14). He was known for mixing "with tax collectors and sinners" (see Lk 7:24), yet he also related to

---

80 *Pastores dabo vobis*, n. 21.

Pharisees[81], synagogue officials[82] and Roman Centurions.[83]

The overriding sense one has of the relationships that Christ formed with diverse people was that of a deep compassion fueled by an understanding of the real human struggles that they experienced. Put simply, Christ loved people, personally, in the concrete reality of their lives. This then is the model for priestly pastoral charity.

Yet Christ was also firm and at times he confronts hardness of heart and hypocrisy. He did not accommodate sin. His relationship with people was always to effect change in their lives: "go, and sin no more" (Jn 8:11). His constant concern was that they could re-orient their lives around an abiding trust and faith in God. He sought conversion of life which would result in a new way of living inspired by a love of God. His initial message – "Repent for the Kingdom of God is close at hand" (Mt 4:17) – never ceased to be the underpinning of all that he said and did during his public ministry.

A priest seeks to exercise his ministry "after the heart of God" and the model for this is the public ministry of Christ. The pastoral life of the priest is formed around his pastoral involvement with his people. Indeed, the heart of a priest is being constantly touched by his exposure to people and the joys and struggles of their lives. He seeks to be an instrument of the love that God has for them. He seeks also to be a means by which they can discover this love of God and be brought to a conversion of life. Like Christ, a priest will also not accommodate evil and sin, and will, as an expression

---

81 While the New Testament tends to comment on Jesus' criticism of the attitudes and practices of the Pharisees, he had a number of personal contacts with them. Notably he had private conversations with Nicodemus (Jn 3:1-21) and there was the occasion where Jesus had a meal at Simon the Pharisee's house (Lk 7:36-50).
82 The compassion that Jesus showed towards Jairus, described by St Luke as a synagogue official is a good example (see Lk 8:40-56).
83 The cure of the Centurion's servant told by St Matthew (Mt 8:5-13) illustrates the fact that the Lord was not only concerned for his own people.

of pastoral charity, seek to bring each person to a new and deeper knowledge of and faith in God.

Obedience

The priest is inspired by the example of Christ in his pastoral relationships. At the same time he seeks to model his character around the character of Christ. One can identify some key defining virtues evidenced in Christ.

One that deserves special consideration is obedience. The New Testament makes a great deal of this virtue. The *Letter to the Hebrews* speaks of Christ "learning to obey through suffering" (Heb 5:8) and refers to Christ as the obedient servant and son who can say, "Here I am, I have come to do your will".[84] St Paul mentions the obedience of Christ many times and contrasts it with the disobedience of Adam. Obedience "unto death"[85] is simply the means by which the effects of the sin of Adam are reversed.[86]

The Lord himself has a clear sense of the fact that his life is one of complete obedience to the will of his Father: "I have not come to do my own will, but to do the will of my Father" (Jn 6:38). This comes into stark contrast in Gethsemani when Christ cries out, "Father, if it be possible let this chalice pass me by" (Mk 14:36), but the Lord moves to his position of surrender to his Father's will, "but not my will, but yours be done". This is a poignant moment: the virtue of obedience rises above human fear. Obedience is a letting go of a desire to control our destiny and entrusting it into the hands of God. The words of the Lord

---

84 See Heb 10:7. Here the author is quoting from Ps 40:6-8, highlighting the fact that the sacrifice truly pleasing to God is that which is from the heart.

85 See Phil 2:6-11. St Paul emphasizes that we ought to have the same mind as that of Christ who humbled himself in obedience to his Father's will even to death.

86 St Paul writes of this in Romans, chapter 5, and draws the comparison between the disobedience of Adam bringing sin into the world and the obedience of Christ being the means of our redemption.

at his last express this: "Into your hands I commend my spirit"
(Lk.23:46).

Obedience is an evangelical virtue, that is, a virtue directly linked
to the Gospel. This particular virtue, in a mysterious way, takes us
to the heart of the salvific work of God in Christ. Obedience
is the pathway for the redeeming action of Christ manifested on
Calvary.

For a priest, obedience is a virtue he accepts. At his ordination
he is asked by his bishop: "Do you promise respect and obedience
to me and my successors?" It means, as every priest knows, that his
future is not solely determined by his own particular preferences.
He places his future in the hands of his bishop. It is the bishop
who will appoint him to particular parishes. It is the bishop who
will ask him to take on certain tasks. Decisions made about him
may not always be his preference, but the priest accepts this fact
in a spirit of submission to God, through the decisions of his
bishop.

Obedience is more than just a willingness to be co-operative.
When fully embraced at the level of Christian virtue it becomes a
participation in the salvific work of God. Obedience is connected
to the will of God. A willingness to embrace an attitude of
obedience opens one's life to the potential of the will of God
being fully realised in our lives. We make ourselves more malleable
in the hands of the master Potter.[87] The prophet Isaiah reminds us
that God's ways are not our ways and his thoughts are high above
our thoughts.[88] An obedient heart provides the context for God's
purposes to be realised in ways that we could never have imagined.
A spirit of obedience and an openness to God's will open us to the
possibility of the plans and purposes of God being carried out in
and through us and taking the fruitfulness of our lives to heights
that we could never imagine.

---

87 See Jer 18:1-11.
88 See Is 55:8.

The virtue of obedience is a pliability and responsiveness that is captured in what can be the prevailing disposition of our hearts: "Here I am, I come to do your will".

Poverty

"The Son of Man has nowhere to lay his head" (Lk 9:58). While not called to the radical poverty expressed in religious life, the evangelical virtue of poverty espoused in the teaching of Christ beckons every priest. Poverty for a priest is principally a matter of developing a genuine spirit of detachment from material things. Such detachment brings a docility of spirit and an inner freedom to the priest. While "the workman deserves his wages" (Lk.10:7) and "those who proclaim the Gospel should get their living by the Gospel" (1 Cor 9:14), a priest needs to guard against any tendency to seek advantage from his pastoral work. This can be a subtle thing, and a true detachment is the key to avoiding erring in this area. Living a spirit of detachment will enable a priest to "travel light" through the years of his ministry, remembering the teaching of the Lord to take neither "haversack nor sandals" (Lk 10:4).

The Lord clearly identified with the poor. The priest must have a heart for the poor. The Vatican Council taught on this matter, "Priests, following the example of Christ, who, rich though he was, became poor for love of us – should consider the poor and the weakest as people entrusted in a special way to them, and they should be capable of witnessing to poverty with a simple and austere lifestyle, having learned the generous renunciation of superfluous things".[89]

> The interior freedom which is safeguarded and nourished by evangelical poverty will help the priest to stand beside the underprivileged; to practice solidarity

---

89 *Optatam Totius,* n. 9; see also *Code of Canon Law,* can. 282.

with their efforts to create a more just society; to be more sensitive and capable of understanding and discerning realities involving the economic and social aspects of life; and to promote a preferential option for the poor. The latter, while excluding no one from the proclamation and gift of salvation, will assist him in gently approaching the poor, sinners and all those on the margins of society, following the model given by Jesus in carrying out his prophetic and priestly ministry.[90]

This virtue fostered in the life of the priest will assist him in the proper administration of the goods of the Church. He will see the material goods of the parish as belonging to the community and not his own. He will have a consideration for the needs of the community and allow parishioners to access the facilities of the parish. The priest will have a keen sense of propriety and honesty in all dealings with the resources placed under his responsibility.

This virtue also fosters a spirit of communal concern. As in the *Acts of the Apostles* where the goods were all held in common,[91] the goods of the Church under his administration will be seen as for the wider good of the Church. The priest then will be conscious of ensuring an equitable distribution of resources, especially ensuring that his parish assists other parishes or works of the Church that are in special need.

Such a spirit of detachment and the generous use of the resources available to him, will be a witness to the parish and the wider community of evangelical poverty. This is especially relevant in the consumerist social environment of today.

---

90 *Pastores dabo vobis,* n. 30.
91 See Acts 2:42-47.

Service

Jesus of Nazareth is God made man. God the Son, "dwelling in unapproachable light",[92] has emptied himself of his divine prerogatives and taken on the condition of a creature. The immensity of what has occurred in the Incarnation is often overlooked because it is a truth so familiar to us. St Paul sought to capture this in a hymn in his letter to the Philippians. He describes Christ as taking on "the condition of a slave" in being born in human likeness.[93] The Apostle goes on to say that he was prepared to humble himself further and became "obedient unto death, even death on a cross".

This self-emptying is technically called the *kenosis*. It captures a key aspect of the Christian mystery. God has laid aside his rightful prerogatives so that he might be completely one with us in order to save us. The humility of God in Christ is revealed in the chosen circumstances of his birth and early life – born in a stable, forced into exile, living in obscurity for some thirty years. This is how God has chosen to reveal himself, not by an awesome display of power and the demand for submission to him, but rather by being willing to come among his creatures in humble simplicity.

Jesus would comment on his view of his life among men, "The Son of man came not to be served, but to serve, and to lay down his life for many" (Mk 10:45). In this Jesus has established a precedent for all those who follow him, especially those chosen ones. At the Last Supper he illustrated this as he laid aside his outer garments to kneel at the feet of his disciples and wash them. When Peter protested that he should not be doing this, Jesus called on his disciples to imitate what he had just done.[94]

Those in leadership are called upon to serve. The Lord introduced a new way of viewing leadership: it is to be an act

92 See Eucharistic Prayer IV.
93 See Phil 2:7.
94 See Jn 13:4-14.

of service. "You see how the rulers lord it over ... this must not happen among you..." (Mt 20:25).

This striking revelation of how God acts and how Jesus wants his disciples to act lays a foundation for how a priest sees the nature of his priestly life among the people. He is among them as "one who serves". In a particular way this means that a priest avoids resting on his rights and the privileges of office. A priest, in the spirit of Christ, expects no privilege or favour. He seeks not standing or recognition. He views his life as one of service to the people.

This takes particular expression in his dealings with the poor and suffering. He is content to be among those who have no public position or influence. Like Christ himself he has a special concern for those whom the world rejects or of whom the world thinks little. He is happy in their company and offers his interest and concern for their needs.

This spirit of service is a laying down of one's life for the people in imitation of the Good Shepherd who was prepared to lay down his life for the sheep.[95] A priest's life is *for* the people. He lives to give himself to the people in daily acts of generous service.

This spirit of service which lives in the hearts of priests flies in the face of popular views of leadership. Many who cry out for a stronger role in the decision-making of the Church see it as the exercise of power. There is a perception that priests want to hold on to power. Certainly the role of leadership calls for the exercise of decision-making, but it is a role exercised primarily from a heart and life laid down for the people. The Christian spirit of leadership is one of service.

---

95 See Jn 10:11.

Growing in the Virtues

A priest is called upon daily to embrace of life of virtue. The grace of ordination imparts a sacramental character of priesthood. There is simply a grace at work within the one ordained in Sacred Orders. This grace can flourish as a priest willingly embraces the call to grow in priestly virtue. He walks the path of virtue. He hears daily the call of Christ to live more like him. His soul is washed daily with the Word of God that speaks to his heart about becoming more aligned to the heart of God.

The prophet Jeremiah echoed a stirring promise from God as he looked out on the people lacking true shepherds. "I will give you shepherds after my own heart" (Jer 3:15). The Scriptures reveal that God has a profound concern for the pastoral needs of his people. In no uncertain terms God spoke through the prophet Ezekiel:

> Son of Man, prophesy against the shepherds of Israel; prophesy and say to them, "Shepherds, the Lord Yahweh says this: Trouble for the shepherds of Israel who feed themselves! Shepherds ought to feed their flock...." (Ez 34:1-2).

A priest can hear in the depths of his heart the call of the Lord to him to be the shepherd that God wants and the people need.

Affective maturity

To be this sort of person it is vital that the priest achieves a healthy affective maturity. The ability to receive and give love is the key to a healthy affectivity. In the encyclical *Redemptor Hominis*, Pope John Paul wrote, "Man cannot live without love. He remains a being that is incomprehensible for himself; his life is meaningless, if love is not revealed to him, if he does not encounter love, if he does not experience it and make it his own, if he does not participate intimately in it".[96] Affective maturity is the ability of a person to integrate their entire reality – physical, psychic and spiritual – in a free capacity to give oneself and receive openly love from others.

A key expression of affective maturity is the capacity to enter into healthy relationships with others. A priest needs to have a good range of relationships. A priest can benefit particularly from sound relationships with his own natural family. This environment is of immense assistance to a priest in his celibate life. Ongoing family relationships provide a stability to a priest whose life may involve moving from one parish to another, from one pastoral responsibility to another. A priest has a privileged role in the family. He is son, brother, uncle in a unique way. He celebrates the family baptisms, weddings and funerals. He is respected and honoured. Because he is a priest he is seen as available to the family in a particular way. He can be a confidant, a peacemaker, a source of inspiration and encouragement.

Fraternal relationships with his fellow priests mean that he can share his more specifically priestly experience with those who can understand. He forms special bonds with those with whom he shares his seminary years. His early years in the ministry will bring him into contact with older priests whom he admires and who become formal or informal mentors. Various meetings, groups or associations of priests can provide a rich source of brotherly support. There is a bond among priests that can enable priests to share deeper experiences with one another. Priestly fraternity is a vital source of a healthy affective life.

Relationships with lay people, especially families, provide a rich source of love and encouragement. Priests are trusted and often warmly welcomed into homes and families. They are a welcome guest at the dinner table. Priests are held in high esteem and the people want to reach out to offer them their love and support.

---

96 *Redemptoris Hominis*, n. 10.

Individual friendships are a natural human experience. A priest needs to have such friendships. Friendships are built around common interests. It is healthy for a priest to have interests outside strictly pastoral work – in sport, in a hobby, in the arts. Discovering others of similar interests provides a rich source of human company and the nourishing of the affective life.

A priest is in the position to form a wide range of relationships that colour and enrich his life. He often has the freedom and flexibility to develop such relationships and find in them a refreshment of his human spirit.

Chapter Eight

The living situation of a priest

Not only must seminary formation foster the human and Christian character and the affective maturity of the priest, but the living situation of the priest's life must enable him to grow and flourish as a human being. The question of the living situation of the priest is a timely one. Physical and emotional wellbeing are affected by the conditions that mark our daily life. The question of a healthy daily pattern of life for priests needs special attention these days.

A priest ordained thirty or forty years ago would remember what the life of a priest was like and how it has so radically changed to what it is today. Let us consider particularly the daily pattern of life of a priest as lived in the presbytery.

A typical presbytery in times past would have a parish priest and one or more curates. There was a live-in housekeeper. Meals were at set times. One would come in for breakfast and the table was set. The housekeeper might even prepare some porridge or a hard boiled egg. Lunch was the main meal of the day and served at a set time, 12.30pm or 1.00pm. In the evenings around six o'clock the housekeeper would again have a table set and a lighter meal served. The priests ate together. The young curate learnt not to be late and risk the ire of the housekeeper! Sunday lunch was more formal; perhaps a roast dinner was the order of the day.

The priests ate in the dining room, which had a homely feel. There was a feminine touch in evidence. There was a clean tablecloth. There were flowers in a vase. There were serviettes. The table was nicely set. Butter was in the butter container with its special knife. There was a simple ritual to the meal. Perhaps there was a small bell next to the parish priest to ring when the first course was completed.

Depending on the character of the parish priest there may have been particular occasions when other priests would come for lunch. It may have been the friends of the parish priest, or perhaps the local priests after confessions for the high school students in preparation for First Friday.

The quality of the food was generally good. It may have been plain cooking because that is what the housekeeper knew, but the food was healthy and priests enjoyed a balanced diet.

The presence of the housekeeper meant that the door and phone were covered by her when the priests were eating. Parishioners who bothered the priests at meal times may have got short shrift from a protective housekeeper: "Father cannot be disturbed".

Daily life was well ordered. There was Mass in the parish church at 6.30am or a little later. One priest was rostered for the nuns. The curate had his particular duties: State School catechetics, visitation, the communion round, the youth group, the altar servers training. Life had a predictable pattern. The parish priest had his set routine. The curate had a round of duties to be carried out.

Presbytery life today

All this may be a little nostalgic and perhaps idealised, but the priest's life was structured and there was a pattern to presbytery life that provided a real support to the life of the priest. How times have changed!

In most cases today the parish priest lives alone. Only a couple of major parishes have an assistant priest. If there is another priest living in the presbytery, he often has his own quarters, and where priests share the same house the priests lead individual lives.

It is rare these days to find that there is a live-in housekeeper. In many instances now there is a woman who comes in once or twice a week to clean, and perhaps prepare some meals which are then frozen. The house is kept clean, but the feminine touch is not there as much as before, because the woman who cleans does not live on the premises.

Meals are taken haphazardly. Breakfast is taken in the kitchen while the morning newspaper is read. Lunch is often now not the main meal, or, if it is, it is often eaten alone. The evening meal is had at all sorts of different times, according to what is happening. It is usually from the microwave, and again eaten alone in the kitchen, or more likely in front of the television. The food eaten is often not the most healthy. The priest goes for convenience meals. Mealtimes have become simply functional, and are not social occasions.

A parish priest these days can't really entertain, unless he has a particular gift for entertaining and loves to cook. The presbytery becomes cold and isolating. The priest slips into a bachelor existence. He does not take as much care of himself as he should. He gets used to being alone.

There is a secretary. She answers the phone and the door during the day. But from 5pm the priest must respond to all contact. There can be the tyranny of the phone and door. There is no "first line of defence" so that the priest is protected from being harried by unnecessary intrusions – someone wanting the key to the hall or telling him that the toilet has no toilet rolls.

The daily routine is no longer as predictable as before. The priest is alone responsible for all the pastoral work of the parish. He may have a pastoral assistant who helps particularly with sacramental programmes (which used to be done in the school by the sisters). There are a band of faithful volunteers who carry out all sorts of key jobs in the parish, but there is no peer with whom to share the work and to discuss the day's affairs. Only priests really know what it is like to be a priest. And, there is the burden of administration which seems to be getting more and more demanding.

Daily Mass is now more often than not at 9.00am. On one morning there is a school Mass. The priest is saying more Masses than in previous times because of funerals, monthly Mass in the nursing home and Nuptial Masses on Saturdays. The pattern of life becomes such that the priest gets up for breakfast and heads over for the Mass and then the day runs on with all sorts of demands. There is little structure or pattern. One casualty of this is that prayer goes by the board.

The priest feels harassed and tired. There is too much required of him. His life has become a disordered rush of meeting various demands. He feels frustrated and isolated.

Perhaps this is a little too bleak a picture, and priests do manage better than just depicted, but elements of the above are true of the lives of many priests today. Has the time come for us to stop and consider what is happening to the lives of priests? Is a certain malaise that is evident among priests due not just to the increasing demands of the work, but to the difficulties that priests face today, exacerbated by a lack of pattern and structure to their lives? Has the way of life of priests become debilitating?

History reveals that there have been attempts over the centuries to provide for a healthier life for priests, focussed on a degree of fraternal life. An example would be certain movements among clerics that emerged in the ninth century. It seems that at this time during the Carolingian renewal various efforts were being made to enable clerics to be supported by some degree of common spiritual life.[97]

---

97 See Leclercq, Vandenbroucke, Bouyer, *A History of Christian Spirituality*, vol. II, "The Spirituality of the Middle Ages," pp. 72 -75.

One example of this was a movement for deaneries to meet once a month and there to be included in their meeting a spiritual conference and a time of prayer. Another effort involved confraternities of priests being formed to provide material and spiritual support for clerics. Clearly it was understood that priests needed some form of fraternal support.

In 754, the bishop of Metz, St Chrodegang, drew up a rule for the clergy of his diocese, the *Ordo Canonicus*. As well as providing guidance concerning liturgical life, the main purpose of this rule was to encourage a degree of common life among clerics. They were still to retain their own homes, but there was to be a common refectory. The saintly bishop was inspired by the Rule of St Benedict. He did want to encourage a more complete renunciation of personal property among his priests, but it was not mandatory in the diocese, and simply served as an ideal for his clergy. Bishop Chrodegang understood that his priests needed the support of a fraternal life and saw the value of priests coming together for a common meal.

A council held at Aachen in 817 produced a rule for clerics. It drew upon the teaching of the Fathers: St Gregory, St Isidore, St Augustine, St Jerome, among others. Clerics, in contrast to the monks, were not required to surrender private property nor live an austere life, but they were to have some degree of common life and live in such a way as to be worthy of the sacred mysteries that they celebrated. Rabanus Maurus, (c.776-856, Abbot of Fulda, 822-42; archbishop of Mainz, 847) wrote *De clericorum institutione*.[98] It was a detailed instruction for priests on how to conduct their life and ministry.

We see in these efforts a concern to offer priests a form of priestly life that supported their native ideals – to be pastoral men.

---

98 See PL 107, 293-420.

St Augustine's way of being bishop

In considering this issue of fraternal life for priests the example of
St Augustine of Hippo is very telling. In a homily given to explain
to the people the way of life that he sought to live as bishop, he
commented on his original purposes in coming to Hippo as bishop:
"I, whom you see, by God's grace, as your bishop – I came as a
young man to this city, as many of you know. I was looking for a
place to set up a monastery to live with my brethren".[99] Augustine
came to Hippo looking to the possibility of setting up common
life.

After his conversion to the Catholic faith Augustine had formed
a community life outside Milan among a group of his philosophy
companions. The monastic ideals percolated among the Christians
of this period. Augustine sought a way of embracing some of
the monastic ideals within the context of his own situation as a
philosopher. For Augustine personally there was a strong need
for fraternal companionship. He needed the stimulation and
consolation of living a common life with people of like mind and
intellect!

The bishop, Valerius, preached about the needs of the Church
and the congregation thrust the newly arrived layman, Augustine,
into priesthood and then into the episcopate. As Augustine
describes in an extraordinarily frank sermon, "I was grabbed. I
was made a priest….and from there I became your bishop".[100]
Augustine had established a community life in what has come to
be called, the "monastery in the garden". He invited his friends
to join him in a common life – besides his two close companions,
Evodius and Alypius, he attracted a number of other men to join
him. He referred to himself and his companions as the "servi
Dei", servants of God.

---

99 *Sermon* 355:2.
100 Ibid.

On being raised up to be bishop, Augustine did not want to live alone in his new state. With all the demands upon him as bishop, a fraternal environment was of vital importance to him. He found it refreshed his spirit. After the stresses of his role as bishop, the opportunity to be able to gather with the brethren around the meal table was of the utmost importance to him.

He moved from the "monastery" into the bishop's house. Augustine insisted that his priests live with him in a monastic style of life: with poverty, celibacy and a rule of life. The ideal that he held before him was the description of the life of the early Church as depicted in the *Acts of the Apostles*, chapter 4. The life, while strict, was built around a profound spirit of brotherly love. For Augustine this love was grounded in friendship. He would call a friend, "half of my soul".[101] Table conversation was not to degenerate into gossip and he had inscribed on the table: "Whoever thinks he is able to nibble at the life of absent friends must know that he is unworthy of this table".[102]

The Church would inherit the "Rule of St Augustine". It was initially written to guide a group of consecrated women in Hippo, but wonderfully captures his own spirit, and the desire he had for a form of common life as a cleric. His Rule captures the spirit of the common life he longed to live: "The main purpose for you having come together is to live harmoniously in your house, intent upon God in oneness of mind and heart".[103]

Augustine was a bishop, with all the demands of the role bearing in upon him. He had a simple desire – to live in fraternal harmony with his brother clerics. And so it was in the bishop's house in Hippo. It attracted an extraordinary group of men who would later become bishops in their own right across North Africa.

The example of St Augustine can cause us to consider the way

---

101 *Confessions* IV, vi, ii.
102 See Peter Brown, *Augustine of Hippo*, p. 200.
103 *Rule*, n. 2.

priests live their lives. Chapter 2 of the *Book of Genesis* tells us that as God settled man in the Garden of Eden, he said, "It is not good for man to be alone" (Gen 2: 18). There is a truth here. A man by himself is not a good thing! A priest by himself is not a good thing. Given the circumstances of today, how can the life of a priest be more effectively supported?

Most priests today will, in fact, be living alone. It is far from ideal, but modern circumstances require it. Positive steps need to be taken to provide a more effective human support for the priest.

Celibacy: a call to fraternity

Celibacy is not a call to being alone. It is not intended to place a priest in a life of human isolation. Celibacy is a call to fraternity. It is worth noting that the Lord himself from the very first moments of his public ministry called men to join him as his companions. It was a master/disciple relationship essentially, but it clearly set up a common fraternal life.

There is an important distinction that can be made between friendship and fraternity. Friends are chosen. Friendship is built on a certain natural chemistry of common background and interest. We have friends in the priesthood, often from our seminary days. This is good and human and healthy. Fraternity, on the other hand, is not chosen, but rather it is given. It is those priests with whom we live and work. The attraction is not based on human compatibility, but rather is grounded on the brotherhood of the priesthood, and ultimately on the common spiritual brotherhood of the Christian life. We are brothers in the Lord.

Circumstances beyond ourselves give us these fraternal relationships. A priest is assigned to live in the presbytery with us. At the human level this may prove an easy and happy arrangement, or it may prove a challenging situation. Whatever the natural dimensions of the relationship, the priest seeks to move to another level when he can say, "you are my brother". By the very nature of their lives priests are called to fraternity with one another. This fraternity becomes, then, the basis and inspiration for the way in which priests live as priests.

Presbytery life

Let us return to the question of presbytery life. The priest needs a good human environment in which to live. A priest needs someone to look after the house. Men on the whole are not good at this!

It is very difficult to have a fulltime live-in housekeeper, but a daily (Monday to Friday) part-time housekeeper is a possibility, indeed a necessity. The priest needs to have a properly cooked meal each day. The presbytery needs proper care and cleaning and the laundry needs to be done. The dining room table needs to become the place for meals. There should be flowers on the table, a clean tablecloth, and a butter dish! Food needs to be bought and the larder stocked.

Meals need to be taken in the dining room and not in the kitchen. A housekeeper could set the table for the evening meal and have something ready to be heated or taken from the fridge.

A priest should be in a position to offer hospitality, at least during the day, and particularly for his fellow priests. A housekeeper would enable this to be possible. The presbytery needs to be a home for the priest.

As well as a part-time housekeeper, each presbytery should have the services of a secretary, Monday to Friday. A secretary can take the pressure off having to answer the door and phone, at least during office hours. The secretary can assume many basic tasks associated with the running of the parish and free the priest to concentrate on his specific pastoral work. This is now largely the case in most parishes, but it is a service that is needed five days a week to provide some relief for the priest.

Thus, each parish needs two key people to support the priest: a housekeeper and a secretary. Each priest can then structure his life in a more human way.

Fraternal life

But more is needed than just these two services. Diocesan priests need to change their way of thinking: priests need to take the view that fraternal life among the clergy is the norm, and living alone is the exception. While circumstances force many priests to live alone, it should not be accepted as inevitable and the preferred practice. Fraternal life should be sought. Wherever it is possible, priests should live with other priests. This fraternal life should not just be the functional sharing of a house, but a genuine effort to build a brotherly relationship and some degree of common life should be sought. This common life can be built initially around the table. Meals should be taken together. Priests sharing a house together should give priority to certain, if not all, daily meals during the week being eaten together. Presbyteries should once again become places of hospitality. Opportunities will be taken to welcome other priests.

A further step can be taken. The priests can introduce a simple rule of life. It may include particular times to pray the Divine Office together. It could be a good practice to provide daily Morning Prayer in the church led by a priest. In doing this the priest is provided with a liturgical setting for the saying of the Office and a simple discipline – he needs to be there to lead the Office! This has the simple effect of setting up a pattern to the day.

Pastoral demands must not so dominate the life of a priest that he is not be able to have some structure, a rule of life, that brings a degree of humanity and spirituality to his life.

The ideal starting point for this is the cathedral. It can become the model for the diocese. The bishop with his cathedral priests could commit themselves to develop a simple common, regular life. The common life would centre on their fraternal relationships, expressed through "table fellowship". The regular life would be expressed through the developing of a simple rule of life for daily prayer; for instance, praying the Morning Prayer of the Office together.

St Augustine expressed his struggles and his hopes in these words: "I came to be bishop, and I found it necessary that a bishop should show unwearying kindness to all who called upon him or were passing his way, and if a bishop did not so act he would be called inhuman. But if this custom had been tolerated in a monastery it would have been out of place. And this was why I wished to have with me in this my Episcopal house a community of priests. This then is how we live".[104]

How true it is for all priests! There is no question that the demands on priests are great. Priests need a better way of life than they have at present to enable them to be the priests they desire to be. It is not enough for priests just to go on in a stoic determination to be good priests, when the circumstances of their life are militating against them.

It is not easy to surrender independence. Being alone is attractive in many ways, and at times easier, but priests will pay a price for this aloneness. It is not good for man to be alone! Priests need each other. Priests need some form of common, regular life in order to foster the humanity and spirituality they need in order to be the priests they desire to be.

---

104 *Sermon*, 355.

Chapter Nine

The spiritual life of the priest

The spiritual life of a priest is heavily influenced by the liturgical cycle of the Church's year. The priest "lives" the liturgical year. The liturgical seasons and their particular spirit and colour frame the consciousness of the priest. The Church follows a path each year of recalling and commemorating the birth, ministry, death and resurrection of Christ, against the setting of the whole economy of salvation traced through Judaism and now realised in and through the Church.

So the priest is engaged in living this mystery closely as he celebrates its various moments. Through the Sunday Masses, the daily Masses, the special liturgical moments, the priest is immersed in the mysteries of Christ commemorated through its yearly rotation. He not only leads his community through the liturgical year, but he is also called upon to preach on these mysteries. So the priest reflects, studies, prays over these mysteries and the sacred texts that commemorate them, and he is drawn ever more deeply into their meaning.

The texts of the prayers of the missal, especially the Eucharistic Prayers, the sacramental formulations, the scriptural readings designated for each particular celebration, the psalms and prayers from the Breviary, flow over the consciousness of the priest on a daily basis. His mind and heart are being washed by the liturgical life of the Church. His inner spirit is being coached and moulded. Any priest of a number of years of ministry would have memories of texts, phrases and images that linger deep in his consciousness from this exposure to the Church at prayer.

The daily celebration of Mass also requires the priest to commemorate the life and witness of a variety of saints. Priests will often offer a few comments on the saint of the day, and at times preach specifically on the saint. Again the priest is immersed in the world of the saints. He learns about their lives, reflects on their spirit and is aware of their greatness.

Celebration of Mass

The focus of the priest's spiritual and pastoral life is the celebration of the Mass, the "source and summit" of the Christian life as the *Catechism of the Catholic Church* teaches.[105] It is the "source and summit" of the spiritual life of the priest. Daily Mass is far more than the provision of a service for the people; it is for the priest the moment when he is most a priest. He stands and says the words of the Lord at the Last Supper, "This is my body", "This is my blood". At that moment he is entering the centre of Christian faith, the mystery of the death and resurrection of Christ – for us! He invites the people to profess this faith and they declare, in one of the formulas, "Dying you destroyed our death, rising you restored our life, Lord Jesus come in glory". In these words priest and people recognise that what they are now commemorating and making real for them is the essential act of salvation wrought by Christ.

---

105 The *Catechism of the Catholic Church*, n. 1324: "The Eucharist is the source and summit of the Christian life. The other sacraments, and indeed all ecclesiastical ministries and works of the apostolate, are bound up with the Eucharist and are oriented toward it. For in the blessed Eucharist is contained the whole spiritual good of the Church, namely Christ himself, our Pasch."

The priest each day visits this reality and, while there is the danger of a dulling of awareness because of routine, the priest is drawn into the drama of God's work of salvation. He not only recalls it, but makes it present for himself and the people.

Pondering the Scriptures

A priest is a preacher of the Word of God. It is his first task.[106] Preaching is far more than explanation of a text, or simple moral exhortation, because the Word of God is "something alive and active" (Heb 4:12) and the Word of God is the power of God for the salvation of all who believe (Rom 1:16). Thus, the priest as preacher must be profoundly imbued with the Word of God and deeply aware of its supernatural power and efficacy. He must be open to receive the Word into his own heart and life. He must first be a hearer of the Word of God, so that the words he speaks are not merely human wisdom, but the wisdom of God.[107]

"Each day he listens as a disciple" (Is 50:4-5), the prophet says of the Servant of Yahweh. A priest's life revolves around the contemplation and the proclamation of the Word of God. For the priest quiet meditation on the Word of God is a vital component of his life. Each day he has the Scriptures given to him through the Church in its liturgy. The practice of daily preaching in the Liturgy provides a particular means by which each day the priest sits with the Word, listening to what the Spirit of God is saying firstly to him. From those moments of reflection and quiet attention to the voice of God, he can then speak of "things of the Spirit".

Origen advised, "We must learn to listen to the Word in the

---

106 "It is the first task of priests as co-workers of the bishops to preach the Gospel of God to all men... (so as to)... set up and increase the People of God". Second Vatican Council, Decree *Presbyterorum Ordinis*, n. 4.
107 See 1 Cor 2:17-25.

same way in which it was written: in the Spirit".[108] Indeed, a priest
will preach the Word in the same way in which it was written: "in
the Spirit". The homily is best prepared on our knees!

Breviary

In the *Liturgy of the Hours* the Church offers the "laus perennis",
the continual praise of God. It is the "Prayer of the Church", but
it is in a particular way a priestly prayer. Each priest, in saying the
Divine Office, unites himself with the chorus of praise ascending
to God from the Church. He offers a "sacrifice of praise". The
priest is the man of the Church and in the Divine Office he joins
himself not only with the Church on earth, but also with the
Church in heaven, with the angels and saints, in giving glory and
honour to God. His voice helps build the chorus of praise, the
joyful worship of Him "who was, who is and who is to come"
(Rev 4:8).

The Divine Office is part of the Liturgy of the Church and
as such it is not just personal devotion. However much a priest
may spiritually benefit from his saying of the Divine Office, he
is first and foremost engaging in a liturgical act of the Church.
The efficacy of the prayer goes far beyond the benefit to the
individual.

However, the saying of the Breviary is spiritually enriching
for the individual priest. The psalms have a wonderful potency in

---

108 Pope Benedict spoke of the approach of Origen to reading Sacred Scripture and
commented: "But this sense transcends us, moving us towards God in the light of
the Holy Spirit, and shows us the way, shows us how to live. Mention of it is found,
for example, in the ninth *Homily on Numbers*, where Origen likens Scripture to [fresh]
walnuts: "The doctrine of the Law and the Prophets at the school of Christ is like
this," the homilist says; "the letter is bitter, like the [green-covered] skin; secondly,
you will come to the shell, which is the moral doctrine; thirdly, you will discover the
meaning of the mysteries, with which the souls of the saints are nourished in the
present life and the future" (*Hom. Num.* 9,7). General Audience, 25 April 2007.

touching the daily reality of living a life of faith. Their testimony to the range of human experience and to the quest of the individual soul for union with God invariably engages us with the daily pilgrimage of faith. They will so often bring into clarity and capture accurately the state of our soul.

The discipline of the Divine Office of sanctifying the day at periodic moments – morning, evening and night – ensures that the ebb and flow of the day does not pass without being engaged with a turning to God.

Prayer

Through the sacred actions that make up the daily life of a priest – the Mass, the Breviary, meditation on and preaching of the Word of God – a priest's life is one grounded in prayer. He is to be a man of prayer. Prayer is a critical element in the priest's life. Yet the reality is often difficult!

A priest is conscious of the need to nourish his interior life. It is something he heard constantly during his seminary formation. He knows this truth: that the efficacy of his ministry relies upon the quality of his interior life. Yet priests in the setting of parish ministry find themselves constantly deprived of a pattern to life that engenders interiority and the capacity for serious prayer. The ordered regimen of the seminary has been replaced by a somewhat chaotic daily existence with constant demands being made of him – the phone and door! It is tempting to see one's work as one's prayer. Yet a priest knows that there is no real replacement for times of quiet set aside to be with God.

The Lord himself gives eloquent witness to the fact that busy engagement with people needs to be countered by withdrawal to solitude. Jesus urged his disciples, when he noticed how busy they were becoming, to "come away and rest awhile" (Mk 6:31). Jesus himself would withdraw to be alone to pray (Mk 1:35). He would spend all night in prayer (Lk 6:12).

St Mark explained that when Jesus chose his disciples they were to be "his companions" (Mk 3:13). A disciple must first be with the Master. A priest, acting in the name of Christ, must have as a priority to be with his Lord. There can be no replacing of time given over to being with Christ in prayer.

Despite all this very obvious witness and a personal conviction that prayer is important, priests often struggle to maintain a solid life of prayer. It is true that unless the first hours of the day, before breakfast, are set aside for prayer, it is unlikely that the priest will be able to set aside appropriate time for prayer during the day.

The priest has to work hard to avoid the dangers of pure activism. Prayer must permeate the daily activity of the priest. Indeed the very ministry of the priest can be the source of his spiritual nourishment. A priest who fosters prayer and devotion among the people and participates with them in these activities has a ready source for time devoted to prayer. Thus, a priest could schedule times of Adoration of the Blessed Sacrament, and resolve to avail himself of this time to pray, not just exposing the Blessed Sacrament and returning later for the Benediction.

Making oneself available for confessions can be a useful way of avoiding endless activity. Sitting quietly in the confessional, the priest can say his Office or do some spiritual reading waiting for penitents.

The practice of a monthly day of recollection is worthy of consideration. Visiting a religious retreat centre for a day can be a simple means to provide a real opportunity for prayer. It is something that needs to be placed ahead of time in the diary. There is no reason why one cannot arrange a regular meeting with God! Having a confessor to whom ones goes on a regular basis can allow for some spiritual direction, and provide a source of accountability for one's spiritual life.

Each priest is expected to undertake an annual retreat. Sometimes this week of quiet is a blessed relief from parish demands, and most of the time is taken up with a form of recovery and rest. It is hard to enter effectively into the retreat, but priority should be given to doing a retreat each year. Again it is something that should be placed in the diary at the beginning of the year, before the pastoral demands edge it out.

Fostering the interior life will be a constant challenge for the busy diocesan priest, but it is possible! It is essential!

The basic components of the spiritual life

Priests from their training are well aware of the wisdom of the tradition, as it proposes the basic component elements of the spiritual life. Canon Law, indeed, lists them!

> Clerics have a special obligation to seek holiness in their lives, because they are consecrated to God by a new title through the reception of orders, and are stewards of the mysteries of God in the service of his people.

> §2 In order that they can pursue this perfection:

> 1° they are in the first place faithfully and untiringly to fulfil the obligations of their pastoral ministry;

> 2° they are to nourish their spiritual life at the twofold table of the sacred Scripture and the Eucharist; priests are therefore earnestly invited to offer the eucharistic Sacrifice daily, and deacons to participate daily in the offering;

> 3° priests, and deacons aspiring to the priesthood, are obliged to carry out the liturgy of the hours daily, in accordance with their own approved liturgical books; permanent deacons are to recite that part

of it determined by the Episcopal Conference;

4° they are also obliged to make spiritual retreats, in
accordance with the provision of particular law;

5° they are exhorted to engage regularly in mental
prayer, to approach the sacrament of penance
frequently, to honour the Virgin Mother of
God with particular veneration, and to use other
general and special means to holiness.[109]

The *Directory on the Life and Ministry of Priests* lists the key
components as: "the daily Eucharistic celebration, with adequate
preparation and thanksgiving; frequent confession and spiritual
direction already practiced in the seminary; the complete and
fervent celebration of the liturgy of the hours, on a daily basis;
examination of conscience; mental prayer; divine readings; the
prolonged moments of silence and prayer, above all in periodical
Spiritual Exercises and Retreats; the affectionate expression of
Marian devotions, like the Rosary; the "Via Crucis" and other
pious exercises; and the fruitful reading on lives of the saints".[110]

Each of the elements has a place and a contribution to make
to the quality of the spiritual life of the priest. A priest who sets
out to build his spiritual life on these foundations will be ensuring
that his inner life does not wither over the years, and he will find a
constant source of replenishment of spirit to enable him to serve
his people with undying fervour and joy.

Filial devotion to the Mother of God

For the priest the Blessed Virgin Mary occupies a special place in
his heart and in his spiritual life. Pope John Paul, with his motto

---

109 Can. 276.
110 *Directory on the Life and Ministry of Priests*, n. 39.

"Totus Tuus" – all yours – constantly invoked the Blessed Virgin Mary's maternal care in all his projects, but especially for priests. Speaking to priests he said,

> With tender affection I entrust each of you to the Virgin, given to us in an extraordinary way as Mother of the Eternal Priest. For each of you I place in her clasped hands a humble request for perseverance and for the commitment to leave as a legacy to your brethren at least one who will continue that unique priesthood that lives and springs from love within us.[111]

The Divine Office ends each day with an antiphon to the Blessed Virgin. The priest thus ends his day by turning to the Virgin in filial love. In honouring her thusly, the priest rests his service of her Son and the vicissitudes of the day in her care. He looks to her maternal love to enfold him.

The quiet and steady recitation of the rosary, the appeal of various Marian devotions, the presence of icons honouring the Mother of God, all bring a gentle feminine presence to the life of a priest. He can turn to the "faithful Virgin" who stood at the foot of the cross and place in her care his burdens and pains. He can gaze into the eyes of the "Virgin of Tenderness" and sense her motherly pain for the sufferings of her children. In these moments the heart of the priest is soothed. In a particular way a priest can sense a special communion of spirit with the Virgin Mary. His burden for those to whom he ministers, especially those who have shared their burdens with him, can readily be linked to the maternal heart of Mary, who carries the pain of her children deeply and personally. A priest can sense that Mary understands what he experiences in the daily course of his ministry.

Priests find in the Blessed Virgin one who is a source of comfort and support.

---

111 Message to Priests, 19 June 2000, n. 5.

Holiness

In the end, people want their priests to be holy. They want their priests to witness to and guide them towards a holy life. They want their priest to be a man of God. They can find help in all sorts of ways for other issues in their lives, but the priest is the one who can lead them to God.

Pope John Paul, in *Novo millennio ineunte*, stated, "First of all, I have no hesitation in saying that all pastoral initiatives must be set in relation to *holiness*".[112] He adds, "It is necessary therefore to rediscover the full practical significance of Chapter 5 of the Dogmatic Constitution on the Church *Lumen Gentium*, dedicated to the universal call to holiness". We are being reminded that holiness is the vocation of every Christian. The Pope knows that this call can be seen as too vague and even pious, and comments, " since Baptism is a true entry into the holiness of God through incorporation into Christ and the indwelling of his Spirit, it would be a contradiction to settle for a life of mediocrity, marked by a minimalist ethic and a shallow religiosity"[113]. He reminds us of the radical nature of the Sermon on the Mount: "Be perfect as your heavenly Father is perfect" (Mt 5:48).

In a boldness that we have come to expect of him, Pope John Paul says:

> The time has come to re-propose wholeheartedly to everyone this *high standard of ordinary Christian living*: the whole life of the Christian community and of Christian families must lead in this direction. It is also clear however that the paths to holiness are personal and call for a genuine *"training in holiness"*, adapted to people's needs. This training must integrate the resources offered to everyone with both the traditional

112 *Novo millennio ineunte*, n. 30.
113 Ibid., n. 31.

> forms of individual and group assistance, as well as the
> more recent forms of support offered in associations
> and movements recognised by the Church.[114]

To help the faithful respond to the universal call to holiness proposed to the Church by the Fathers of the Second Vatican Council, priests have a role of being leaders. Holiness in the end means surrendering one's life to God, allowing the Holy Spirit to become the principal agent in our interior life. Holiness in the end is the triumph of the grace of God in us.

---

114 Ibid.

Chapter Ten

The pastoral ministry of the priest

What is the first task of the priest? Many would answer: to say Mass. The Mass is, as the Second Vatican Council document on the Liturgy states, "the source and summit of the Christian life".[115] The Mass is the highpoint of the priest's ministry, but the *first* task of the priest is to proclaim the Gospel. Unless the Gospel is proclaimed there can be no faith, and without faith there will be no one to receive the sacraments.[116]

When Jesus appointed his apostles, the task he assigned to them was to go out and preach. Preaching is the priest's life's work. He preaches to the parish community each Sunday, and to a smaller community at daily Mass. He preaches at sacramental moments – weddings, funerals, baptisms. He has opportunities to preach on a daily basis – to school children, to special apostolic groups in the parish, at functions. Preaching is his life's work.

Preaching

When we come to consider the preaching ministry of the priest we could ask the question: what is the essential message that he is

115 The teaching of *Sacrosanctum concilium*, n. 47, is taken up as the theme for the IX Synod of Bishops, "The Eucharist, Summit and Source of the Life and Mission of the Church".
116 See Rom 10:15.

to preach? Different circumstances will dictate the actual preaching topic and style, but every priest will have a central theme that he sees as *the* message he wants to convey.

There are a number of factors that influence the essential message of preaching. In considering some of these factors we need to keep in mind the question: what is the word God wishes to be conveyed to his people in these days?

The central core of the message will emerge from the priest's own inner journey of faith. It will be forged in and through his pastoral experience. It will be the barometer of his own Christian existence. Preaching will reveal the inner life of the preacher, and the deep and personal convictions that drive his life and ministry. It will emerge as the expression of the way in which the mystery of Christ has come to be realised and incarnated in the life of this particular priest.

This highly subjective realisation must be tested against the testimony of Scripture and the living Tradition of the Church. Preaching certainly cannot become something idiosyncratic. A preacher cannot just preach from himself. He is a servant of the Word and a servant of the Church. A preacher submits himself to the Word of God and relies on grace to take him beyond the limits of himself. He also places himself firmly within the teaching Church and seeks to be a faithful communicator of the dynamic aspect of the Church as it responds to the challenges of the age.

A preacher can truly ask, inspired by the words from the *Book of Revelation*, "What is the Spirit saying to the Churches?"[117] What is the Spirit saying to the Church in our time? There are "signs of the times" that need to be noticed. Modern life in western societies is materially rich, but spiritually poor. Pope John Paul and Pope Benedict have consistently addressed this question. We

---

117 In the *Book of Revelation* the phrase is a theme running through the prophetic words addressed to the seven churches, See Rev 1-3.

are building bigger barns and losing our souls![118] The post-war generation has grown up in a time of peace and great opportunity, yet many articulate and educated Catholics find themselves at odds with the Church, particularly on matters of conscience. The young can have noble aspirations about matters of justice and ecology, yet lack a personal connection with God. The preacher is challenged to offer a word which requires a prophetic edge, calling people to deeper personal faith and an obedience to the Word of God and the teaching office of the Church.

What is being called for at this time in our history and culture is a new look at preaching: the fresh development of *evangelical preaching*.

Evangelical Preaching

St Paul reminds us that "it is not against human enemies that we have to struggle, but against the Sovereignties and the Powers who originate the darkness in this world" (Eph 6:12). Preaching is a way of engaging in the spiritual warfare that engulfs the world. There are strong "prevailing spirits" that infiltrate society and bear in on the Church. Ideologies are powerful. They should not be underestimated.

Given that we no longer live in a culture where the prevailing spirit is that of the Christian faith, we need to look again at the nature of the preaching ministry. We cannot presume that those to whom we preach are immersed in a Christian environment. People today live in a thoroughly secular environment. The preacher needs to preach in such a way that it nurtures faith and draws the hearers to an exposure to the essential elements of the Gospel.

Preaching is an instrument to contend with the prevailing spirit of the age and bring the power of the Word of God to bear on the issues of the day. Preaching is an eminently spiritual task and

---

118 See Lk 12:13-21.

needs to be approached "in the Spirit". St Paul in the passage in
Chapter 6 of his letter to the Ephesians speaks of taking up the
"sword" of the Word of God. The preaching of the Word done
"in the Spirit" enables this sword to be wielded. Paul goes on to
urge the Ephesian community to "pray for me to be given the
opportunity to open my mouth and speak without fear and give
out the mystery of the Gospel of which I am an ambassador"
(Eph 6:19).

Preaching "in the Spirit" is a preaching which is aimed not just
at explaining or exhorting, but at moving hearts. Again we turn
to St Paul, the great preacher to the gentiles. In a deeply personal
and moving introductory section to his first *Letter to the Corinthians*,
Paul admits coming among them "in great fear and trembling"
(1 Cor 2:4). Paul had had a chastening experience at Athens. On
the Aeropagus he had attempted to appeal to the minds of the
philosophers by using rational argument in an attempt to persuade
them about Christ. He attempted to preach "in the flesh" rather
than "in the Spirit". It failed.

He must have done some soul searching on his way down
to Corinth because he tells us that he had learnt his lesson and
resolved to come to this city with the sole intention of proclaiming
the cross of Christ, a "foolishness" in human terms: "the Jews
demand miracles and the Greeks look for wisdom and here we are
preaching a crucified Christ" (1 Cor 1:23). St Paul, however, had
learnt that this is the "power of God to save".

Preaching, even among believers in the Christian assembly,
needs to be such that it unleashes "the power of God to save".
The preacher does not rely on his own strength, certainly on "no
show of oratory or philosophy" (1 Cor 2:1), but upon the power
of God to act in and through him.

Pope Paul VI, in his stirring Apostolic Exhortation, *Evangelii
Nuntiandi*, speaks eloquently of the role of the Holy Spirit in
evangelical preaching.

> It is the Holy Spirit, who, today just as at the beginning
> of the Church, acts in every evangeliser who allows
> himself to be possessed and led by him. The Holy
> Spirit places on his lips the words which he could not
> find by himself, and at the same time the Holy Spirit
> predisposes the soul of the hearer to be open and
> receptive to the Good News.[119]

Priests are being called upon by contemporary conditions to develop an evangelical preaching, even at Sunday Mass. What is under threat today is faith, faith as a personal relationship of trust in God. Preaching cannot be merely instructional, or moralistic or expository – it must seek to engender faith. Thus the preacher looks to the power and presence of the Holy Spirit to be the animating presence in his preaching. The preacher seeks to make himself available to being an instrument of the grace of God. His preaching is no longer his own thoughts or knowledge or insights, but rather he is docile to the prompting of the Spirit.

Preaching and the New Evangelisation

Faced with the rising tide of secularism in Australia, priestly preaching cannot just be limited to sacramental occasions. These opportunities to preach will be the "bread and butter" of our preaching task, but the circumstances of the day call on priests to "go out into the marketplace" in order to preach the Gospel to those who would not otherwise have an opportunity to be exposed to the message of the Gospel through the Church.

The challenge of the call to the New Evangelisation is to be bold and innovative in finding ways to preach the Gospel.

What does such preaching look like? We can identify some distinguishing characteristics.

---

119 *Evangelii Nuntiandi*, n. 75.

1. Preaching in the spirit of the New Evangelisation must focus on the proclamation of the person of Jesus Christ. Pope John Paul II in his first Mass as Pope ended his homily with the words, "Open the Doors to Christ". Pope Benedict indicating his intention to continue the same line of evangelisation ended his homily at his first Mass as Pope with the same words.[120] This is a key distinguishing feature of the New Evangelisation. The message must centre on the person of Jesus Christ and invite a response from the heart. The Catholic Church proposes that life and salvation can be found in a personal acceptance of and adherence to Jesus Christ.

2. Such preaching is profoundly Catholic in its presentation. There is a distinctively Catholic form of evangelisation which has notable differences from other evangelical approaches. There is no aggressive "hard sell". Catholic evangelisation *proposes*, not *imposes*, as John Paul II taught.[121] Catholic evangelisation is imbued with a spirit of love and freedom.[122] Catholic evangelisation naturally offers a distinctive sacramental dimension to the Christian life and engages its rich tradition of prayer and spirituality. Special use can be made of Adoration of the Blessed Sacrament and the promotion of Catholic devotions, for example the Miraculous Medal. These can be effective tools to bring people to Christ.

3. The New Evangelisation and the preaching flowing from it engage with people within the context of their lives. While some approaches in evangelisation may

---

120 Pope John Paul II, *Mass at the beginning of the Pontificate* (22 October 1978); Pope Benedict XVI, *Mass for the inauguration of the Pontificate* (24 April 2005).
121 Pope John Paul II, *Redemptoris Missio:* On the permanent validity of the Church's missionary mandate, n. 39.
122 Cf. Vatican II, *Ad gentes*, nn. 2-5,12; Pope Paul VI, *Evangelii nuntiandi*, n. 26.

invite people to the parish church, a distinguishing feature of the New Evangelisation is that the evangelist meets the people "in the market place." In specific evangelisation activities the evangelist will move out into the community, often using innovative ways to engage with people. Some examples of forms of this engagement with people are: door to door visitation, a coffee tent on the street outside the church, singing in public places, engaging people in conversation in the street, having debates in public locations, handing out medals or holy cards, etc. These activities are eventually intended to draw people to meet Christ in the Catholic Church.

4. The New Evangelisation is a particular fruit of the emergence of ecclesial movements in the Church in recent times. Pope John Paul often acknowledged that they were spearheading this New Evangelisation.[123] Priests can be key instruments in encouraging and supporting the evangelising efforts of these new movements, and at the same time they can learn from them. One of the distinguishing features of the New Evangelisation developed by the various movements is that it is largely driven by committed lay people. The New Evangelisation speaks to the laity in a special way because they are "in the world", and have many opportunities to engage with people through their contacts in everyday life. Priests, though, should work alongside the lay people, each responding in their own way to the call to evangelise.

---

123 Pope John Paul II, Address to the Pontifical Council for the Laity (1 March 1999); see Meeting with Ecclesial Movements (30 May 1998).

We face a great challenge in Australia. Secularisation has made deep inroads into our culture. We priests are only too aware of this! Many, many people live as though God did not exist. Sadly many people are living aimless lives and many young people are being caught up in destructive patterns of living. Our preaching needs to find a new dimension in becoming evangelical in the spirit of the New Evangelisation.

Liturgy and Sacraments

The priest, as we have already said, lives the liturgical cycle of the Church. The liturgy is the daily preoccupation of the priest. One could say that the liturgy, in particular the celebration of the Mass, defines the Catholic priesthood. The priest's ministry finds its essence in the celebration of the Eucharist. The life of the priest flows towards the Eucharist and takes its inspiration from the Eucharist. All that the priest does in the parish, even the most mundane, is directed towards the Eucharistic celebration. He brings his own priestly life to its full realisation and meaning when he celebrates Mass with and for the people.

The priest, then, finds in the Mass a daily impetus for his life and ministry as a priest. He is nourished in his identity and his unique role and service to the Christian community when he celebrates Mass. He goes forth to live out his priesthood, which has been wonderfully captured and realised at the altar.

The *Directory on the Life and Ministry of Priests* expresses it thusly:

> The sacramental memorial of the death and Resurrection of Christ, the true and efficacious representation of the singular redemptive Sacrifice, source and apex of Christian life in the whole of evangelisation, the Eucharist is the beginning, means, and end of the priestly ministry, since all ecclesiastical

ministries and works of the apostolate are bound
up with the Eucharist and are directed towards it.
Consecrated in order to perpetuate the Holy Sacrifice,
the priest thus manifests, in the most evident manner,
his identity.[124]

A priest is aware that his life, mission and identity are all
captured in the act of celebrating the Mass. One could say that
the priesthood is derived from the Mass and that the priesthood
exists for the Mass. Priests are the ones who are instrumental in
effecting this "mystery of faith" and enabling the People of God
to be engaged with the salvific action of Christ, sacramentally
made present at every Mass.

A pastoral imperative exists in relation to the celebration of
the Mass. It is not enough that a Mass is celebrated. The priest has
the pastoral task of ensuring that each Mass becomes a worthy
expression of Catholic faith and is spiritually nourishing for the
people. Thus, a priest gives great attention to all aspects of the
celebration of Mass – from ensuring that the church itself is
a "house of prayer" to forming all those involved in the Mass.
The priest's personal preparation for the celebration of Mass is
most important, including time given to preparing the homily and
personal spiritual preparation for each Mass.

Pope Benedict commented on the importance of the priest not
only personally engaging himself and all his spiritual powers in the
celebration of each Mass, but also being, in the end, a vehicle of
the tradition of the Church in its celebration of the mysteries of
the faith. He expressed it thus:

> The *ars celebrandi* is the fruit of faithful adherence to
> the liturgical norms in all their richness; indeed, for two
> thousand years this way of celebrating has sustained
> the faith life of all believers, called to take part in the

---

124 *Directory on the Life and Ministry of Priests*, n. 48.

celebration as the People of God, a royal priesthood, a
holy nation (cf. 1 Pet 2:4-5, 9).[125]

A priest is deeply conscious that the Mass is an act of worship
of the Church and is not to be subject to his own idiosyncrasies.
He faithfully adheres to the direction of the liturgy proposed
authoritatively by the Church. Pope Benedict comments further:

> As a result, priests should be conscious of the fact
> that in their ministry they must never put themselves
> or their personal opinions in first place, but Jesus
> Christ. Any attempt to make themselves the centre of
> the liturgical action contradicts their very identity as
> priests. The priest is above all a servant of others, and
> he must continually work at being a sign pointing to
> Christ, a docile instrument in the Lord's hands. This is
> seen particularly in his humility in leading the liturgical
> assembly, in obedience to the rite, uniting himself to
> it in mind and heart, and avoiding anything that might
> give the impression of an inordinate emphasis on his
> own personality.[126]

At the heart of the priest's life is not only the daily celebration of the
Mass, but also the many times when he celebrates the sacraments.
The sacramental moments for the people are also occasions when
the manner of celebration by the priest has profound significance
for the faith of the people. Sacraments are channels of grace.
They effect real change in the person. The grace communicated
can be not just momentary and passing, but abiding. Some of the
sacraments ensure a transformation of the person by means of
the permanent character wrought by the sacrament. The person is
different after receiving the sacrament. There is a real ontological
change in the person.

---

125 *Sacramentum Caritatis*, n. 38.
126 *Ibid.*, n. 23.

The priest by means of effective catechesis, appropriate preparation and celebration of the sacrament can ensure that the recipients are fully engaged with what is occurring in a hidden but real way within them.

The Day of the Lord

One of the significant changes that has occurred in society in recent decades has been the change in attitudes to Sunday as a day of rest. We have witnessed the growing practice of shopping centres opening on Sundays. We are seeing increasing use of Sunday mornings for sporting competitions. Pope John Paul addressed this issue in his letter, *Dies Domini,* arguing, among other reasons, for the simple human need for a day of rest.

He comments on this in *Novo millennio ineunte* when he speaks of the need to emphasise that "particularly *the Sunday Eucharist* and *Sunday* itself [be]experienced as a special day of faith, the day of the Risen Lord and of the gift of the Spirit, the true weekly Easter".[127]

> For two thousand years, Christian time has been measured by the memory of that first day of the week (Mk 16:2,9; Lk 24:1; Jn 20:1), when the Risen Christ gave the Apostles the gift of peace and of the Spirit (cf. Jn 20:19-23). The truth of Christ's Resurrection is the original fact upon which Christian faith is based (cf. 1 Cor 15:14), an event set at the centre of the mystery of time, prefiguring the last day when Christ will return in glory.[128]

Participating in the celebration of the Eucharist should be, in the

---

127 *Novo millennio ineunte*, n. 35.
128 *Ibid.*

Pope's words, *"the heart of Sunday* for every baptised person".[129]

Pope John Paul has given a timely reminder to the Church that Sunday in the Christian tradition is the "Day of the Lord". In the increasing commercialisation of Sundays, this notion of the special nature of the day is being lost. Even apart from the important spiritual considerations, Sunday does need to be restored as, at least, a day of rest. To make Sunday much as any other day places enormous demands on people. Many are forced to work and lose opportunities for family life and activities. There is the possibility that the Church, in appealing for a restoration of Sunday as a day of rest will find many voices supporting the proposal.

Parish Community

The parish is the normal ecclesial environment for the Catholic and is the location of the celebration of key moments in the pilgrimage of faith through life. Each Catholic holds deep memories of parish life. It is the place of Baptism and Confirmation, of the receiving of First Holy Communion (and First Reconciliation). It is the place for the celebration of the Sacrament of Marriage, and the place from which a Catholic is taken for Christian burial.

The parish community is a key location for formation in our faith. In Australia parishes have supported and developed a very impressive system of primary schools. The parish priest has oversight for the work of the school.

Formation in faith is also provided for adults in a wide variety of ways in the parish. The Sunday homily is an immediate source not only of spiritual nourishment, but also of the ongoing formation of understanding of the faith. Various groups meet in the parish and offer formation in Catholic faith; e.g., Lenten groups, prayer groups, Bible study groups.

The parish is also the place where Catholics receive the

---

129 *Ibid.*

encouragement from other members of the community to live out the faith in the very secular and at times unfriendly environment of contemporary society. Society has significantly changed in recent decades and the influence of Christian culture has diminished. The parish community becomes increasingly the key location for support in living Christian ideals. The witness of fellow parishioners, their example, is increasingly important to the average Catholic. Participating even at the most basic level of attending Mass is an occasion of being united with people who believe what Catholics believe and seek to live as true followers of Jesus Christ and as members of the Catholic Church. Life lived in society offers so few inspirations to Christian ideals. Catholics today can feel isolated and alone in what they believe and how they want to live. The parish community is a welcome refuge and an encouragement for such a Catholic.

A parish is essentially a community of the faithful. The strength of a parish is the quality of the life of the members of the parish living and co-operating together. Parishioners can discover a basic biblical truth: we are brothers and sisters to each other in Christ. Because of the common Baptism and the life of the Spirit that Catholics share, "we belong to one another", as St Paul says (Rom 12:5). Today, more than ever, the Catholic faithful need each other.

The parish, too, needs the contribution of its members and the gifts of each to enable the community to function. Any priest would be only too aware of how much he relies on parishioners for the celebration of the Mass. The priest is reliant upon people to prepare and look after the church, for altar servers and acolytes, for readers and extraordinary ministers, for musicians and singers, for the collectors. He needs the community to participate with him in joining in responses and singing. The parish is a living community, a dynamic reality, which operates effectively when parishioners contribute. St Paul's image of the Church as the Body of Christ, where each member is a different part has ready application to the parish.

A diocesan priest's life is oriented around the service of a parish community. Canon Law (Canon 515) describes the parish as a specific community of the *christifideles* "established on a stable basis within a particular Church". Despite the many social changes, including the growth of large urban centres, the mobility of people, and the increasingly complex and busy life of people, the parish remains the basic cell in the life of the Church.

The history of the development of parishes in the life of the Church is yet to be written. The early Christian communities were overseen by elders, later identified as bishops. As early as the second century local Christian communities were called, in Greek, *paroikia*, translated as "those living near or beside".[130] It also had a secondary meaning depicting "resident aliens", that is, people living in exile. The term captured the notion of the Christian community living in the midst of the world.

The story of the role of the parish under the care of a presbyter shows the need for bishops to entrust communities, either in larger urban centres or in country districts to priests when it was impossible for the bishop to supervise personally the life of the community. With the Peace of Constantine (313 AD) and increasing recognition given to the Church numbers of Christians increased significantly and more individual parish communities became necessary to meet the needs of the people. By the sixth century the terminology concerning Christian communities was more or less settled: the bishop had responsibility for a diocese and priests had pastoral responsibility for the local community of the parish.

People develop great loyalties to their parish community because it is the place where they have lived their Catholic life and

---

130 See James A Coriden, *The Parish is Catholic Tradition*, p. 19.

celebrated its important moments. This is no more in evidence than when a loss of a resident priest or a form of partnering may be required.

In *Christifideles laici,* there is a reflection on the theological identity of a parish. Pope John Paul II acknowledges that while the Church always has a universal dimension, it "finds its most immediate and visible expression in the parish".[131] People experience what it means to belong to the Church, above all, in terms of their relationship with the parish community in which they live.

Pope John Paul II expresses the hope that "in the light of faith all rediscover the true meaning of the parish, that is, the place where the very mystery of the Church is present and at work".[132] He stresses that "the parish is not principally a structure, a territory, or a building, but rather "the family of God, a fellowship afire with a unifying spirit", "a familial and welcoming home", the "community of the faithful". Plainly and simply the parish is founded on a theological reality, because it is a *"Eucharistic community"*.[133] The Pope adds:

> This means that the parish is a community properly suited for celebrating the Eucharist, the living source for its upbuilding and the sacramental bond of its being in full communion with the whole Church. Such suitableness is rooted in the fact that the parish is a *community of faith* and an *organic community,* that is, constituted by the ordained ministers and other Christians, in which the pastor – who represents the diocesan bishop – is the hierarchical bond with the entire particular Church.[134]

---

131 *Christifideles laici,* n. 26.
132 *Ibid.*
133 *Ibid.*
134 *Ibid.*

The parish is entrusted to a parish priest as its shepherd under the authority of the diocesan bishop. A parish only has juridical meaning when it is led by a priest in communion with the bishop.

A parish is an "organic communion between the common priesthood of the faithful and the ministerial priesthood; of fraternal and dynamic collaboration between pastors and faithful, with absolute respect for the rights, duties and functions of both, and mutual recognition of their respective proper competence and responsibility".[135]

This "old and venerable structure"[136] of the parish has an indispensable mission in the midst of all the vast changes in social structures in modern societies. Simply the parish seeks to create the basic community of the Christian people. It is established to initiate and gather the people through a liturgical and sacramental life. It is a key means for people of faith to be nourished and strengthened in that faith. The parish also exists to give expression to a practical and humble charity of good works, and of loving service to the sick and suffering.

Continuing to follow the thought of Pope John Paul in *Christifideles laici*, a "theology of parish" can be built around the ecclesiology of *communion* which was, as the Pope notes, a key concept in the conciliar documents. He quotes the words of Pope Paul VI at the conclusion of the Council: "The Church is a *communion*". Pope John Paul considers that *"The reality of the Church as Communion is,* then, the integrating aspect, indeed *the central content of the 'mystery',* or rather, the divine plan for the salvation of humanity".[137]

For the priest this theological consideration can give quite specific meaning to what his daily life entails. He is a "man of

---

135 *Priest, Pastor and Leader of the Parish Community*, n. 18.
136 Pope John Paul II quotes Pope Paul VI in an address to the Roman Clergy (24 June 1963).
137 *Christifideles laici*, n. 26.

communion". His role as pastor is one of forming the parish as a community.

Collaborative Ministry

The ecclesiology of communion provides a basis for considering the wide diversity of gifts and charisms among those who make up the parish community. St Paul describes the Church analogously as a human body where each member contributes to the whole. Each member of the parish community can be envisioned as possessing certain qualities or gifts that contribute to the parish bringing about its organic completeness. In the years following the Second Vatican Council we have witnessed new levels of participation of parishioners in the life of the parish. It has been one of the great fruits of the Council.

It is the clear teaching of the Church that the lay person has a right and duty to participate in the life of the Church at the parish level. Pope John Paul teaches this very clearly in *Christifideles laici*:

> The Church's mission of salvation in the world is realised not only by the ministers in virtue of the Sacrament of Orders but also by all the lay faithful; indeed, because of their Baptismal state and their specific vocation, in the measure proper to each person, the lay faithful participate in the priestly, prophetic and kingly mission of Christ. The Pastors, therefore, ought to acknowledge and foster the ministries, the offices and roles of the lay faithful that find their *foundation in the Sacraments of Baptism and Confirmation,* indeed, for a good many of them, *in the Sacrament of Matrimony.*[138]

The interrelationship between priest and lay person in the parish is described in terms of "collaborative ministry". The notion can be

---

138 *Christifideles laici,* n. 23.

traced back to the Council's document on the laity:

> The parish offers an outstanding example of the
> apostolate on the community level, inasmuch as it brings
> together the many human differences found within its
> boundaries and draws them into the universality of the
> Church. The lay faithful should accustom themselves to
> working in the parish in close union with their priests,
> bringing to the Church community their own and
> the world's problems as well as questions concerning
> human salvation, all of which need to be examined
> together and solved through general discussion. As
> far as possible the lay faithful ought to collaborate in
> every apostolic and missionary undertaking sponsored
> by their own ecclesial family.[139]

This term, "collaborative ministry", now designates the
character of the relationship between priest and people, and
captures the spirit of close co-operation and mutuality in parish
communities.

The burden of the pastoral office

We have spoken already of the significant changes that have
affected the way in which priests carry out their ministry. There is
clear evidence that priests are finding the pastoral responsibilities
of "running" a parish a burden. Many things, as we have noted,
have changed. More is demanded of the priest while at the same
time, there are fewer priests. Not only may a priest be asked to be
pastorally responsible for more than one community, but whereas
before a priest may have had an assistant, now most priests are
alone. They are the beginning and end of all that happens in the
parish.

It is an appropriate moment to step back a little and examine

---

139 *Apostolicam Actuositatem*, n. 10.

the question of how priests can be better supported in their role. Priests need to be freed to be able to concentrate on the key focus of their ministry – the preaching and sacramental ministry and the pastoral care of their community.

As in most aspects of life today there is an increasing complexity of organisation and increased levels of "compliance" required. One of the most obvious areas of support for the priest is to provide him with administrative support. Every parish should have a secretary, present five days a week. A secretary needs to be trained in parish administration and capable of handling many of the day-to-day administrative tasks associated with parish life.

A priest needs support in the financial management of the parish. The Parish Finance Committee can provide advice to the priest, but he also needs a business manager who at least works on a part time basis. The business manager, as well as managing the finances, can cover other issues like maintenance, which can become a great burden for a priest. A competent business manager could free the priest from the many daily irritations of practical administration.

A priest also needs pastoral assistance. The most obvious need is in the preparation for the sacraments. Such assistance could be part time, and may include additional work in areas like pastoral care of the sick and support for the work of catechists. Another area that needs serious attention is pastoral support in the area of ministry to young people. This area was often in the past the role of the assistant priest, and a priest as lone pastor often has not the time and energy to devote to this very important ministry.

Finally a priest needs assistance in the area of the liturgy. A capable acolyte could assist in the conducting of liturgical and sacramental occasions; e.g., funerals and marriages. A priest should not conduct sacraments alone. He needs to be supported practically and thus freed to concentrate on his pastoral and spiritual role. A priest may need someone to recruit and train and organise altar servers. Key liturgical events should have the services of liturgical ministers. Some assistance in the area of music would also free the priest from concerns and demands made of him in this area.

Too many times priests are left alone to manage the great variety of aspects of parish life. Thus the burden falls on them. While it may be true that many parishioners are keen to assist, we have reached a stage where more professional help for priests is what is particularly required. Left on their own they feel the strain and perform in a less than optimal fashion. In the early Church the apostles felt the pressures of their ministry and resolved it by appointing deacons. In a similar way there is a need to seriously examine the structures of the parish and develop effective ways to support priests. The current situation cannot continue as it is. Priests are flagging under the tasks expected of them. There may need to be a re-ordering of priorities whereby increasing financial support is given to establishing various paid positions in the local parish.

What could a medium to large parish or a partnered parish situation look like in terms of personnel? The parish staff could consist of:

- Parish Priest
- Parish Secretary (five days a week)
- Business Manager (One or two days a week)
- Liturgical assistant (part-time)
- Sacramental Co-ordinator (part-time)
- Youth minister (part-time)

This may seem beyond the scope of the financial resources of many parishes, but if the needs of the priest are presented to the parishioners and if parish budgeting is restructured it is not impossible. It could be possible that deaneries could co-operate to put a number of these strategies in place. For example, a deanery could employ a business manager for a number of parishes. A parish priest could then more effectively co-ordinate the works of the parish through this staff and begin to re-structure his life to focus on his spiritual and pastoral service – seeking to be a shepherd of the flock.

Shepherd

How can a priest best envisage the nature of his relationship with the people he serves in the parish? We have already considered a number of images of the priest – man of God, spiritual father, man set apart.

There is one image that is most appropriate when considering the role of the priest in the parish – the priest as shepherd. It is certainly a description of himself that Jesus prized particularly. On the popular level he was happy to describe himself under the enigmatic title, "son of man". Yet the image of himself as shepherd captured much of how Jesus viewed himself and his ministry.

While some may view this concept of the priesthood as patronising or out of date, it remains an eminently scriptural and appropriately spiritual way of seeing the pastoral role of the priest in the parish. It is not meant to be in any way an elitist or superior approach to the relationship with people. Rather, it reflects the fact that the priest does incarnate the shepherding role of Christ. It is in the name of Christ and in the authority of Christ, that the priest is pastor or shepherd.

He has a task entrusted to him to lead the community. He has a responsibility to preach and teach in the name of Christ and the Church. He is looked to by the people as a spiritual guide. He is given the title, "Father" as a sign of respect and affection and an acknowledgement of his spiritual role in people's lives.

Priests can be tempted to shy away from such a view of their ministry. Some can prefer to be called by their first names and want to dress in secular ways. They may prefer to see themselves as a fellow traveller, rather than a leader. They may wish to pass over responsibility to significant lay leaders or parish councils.

This is not how Christ or the Church views their role and responsibility. Christ clearly entrusted his apostles with spiritual authority.[140] Priests are called to act not only in the name of Christ but in *persona Christi capitis*, in the person of Christ the Head. They are to take up the mantle of being shepherds prepared to lay down their lives for the sheep.[141]

Such a priest, as a "good shepherd", is then a priest "after the heart of God".[142]

---

140 In sending out his disciples to preach and heal in his name Jesus, St Matthew tells us, "gave them authority" (Mt 10:1). At the Ascension Jesus gave his apostles the Great Commission beginning with the solemn words, "All authority in heaven and earth has been given to me" (Mt 28:18)

141 In the great passage where Jesus depicts himself as the Good Shepherd, the high point of the teaching is that the Good Shepherd is one who is prepared to lay down his life for his sheep (Jn 10:11).

142 Samuel's description of David in 1 Sam 13:13-14 is the finest compliment a priest as pastor could be given!

Chapter Eleven

The future of the priesthood

The seedbed for a new type of seminarian

There is a new spirit of convinced faith emerging among many young Catholics. There is a growing cohort of young people finding a deep conviction about their Catholic faith. For some their faith is firmly established by an intellectual conviction about the truth of Catholic teaching. Many of these young people are the 'spiritual sons and daughters' of Pope John Paul who now embrace Pope Benedict as their mentor. They tend to be well versed in Catholic teaching and have a thirst to grasp more of the faith. They are critical of any effort to accommodate the faith to contemporary culture and they see themselves as firmly counter-cultural. They are committed not only to clear theological positions, but they are also strongly aligned with the Church's teaching on ethical issues, especially in the area of bioethics.

Others have come to a new-found faith through involvement in one of the many new ecclesial movements in the Church. In some cases, their faith has a marked evangelical spirit linked with a strong desire to be fully Catholic. These young Catholics have an evangelistic outlook. Theirs is a joyful appreciation of the Christian life grounded in a love of the Scriptures and a desire to enter into the worship of God reflected in contemporary forms of Christian music. They are drawn to prayer and new forms of Christian community.

This new generation of convinced Catholics have been called the "new devout".[143] Colleen Carroll, author of *The New Faithful*, quotes Peter Kreeft as saying that there is a new generation of young Catholics who reject "the old, tired, liberal, modern" view of life.[144] It is as though they are emerging from a fog of uncertainty and want something solid and clear upon which they can build their lives.

Carroll summarises some of their defining qualities. She comments that they establish their identity centred around their religious beliefs, and they develop their moral views from their beliefs. Their worldview challenges many core values of the dominant secular culture. They are willing to embrace challenging faith commitments that offer them firm guidelines on how to live their lives. They have no fear of experiencing rejection because of their adherence to traditional morality and religious devotion. She comments that they "seek guidance and formation from legitimate sources of authority and trust these authorities to help them find lasting happiness and avoid repeating their own painful mistakes or those of their parents and peers". This generation strives for "personal holiness, authenticity and integration in their spiritual lives".[145]

A new type of seminarian

Vocations are coming from this new spirit of faith among young Catholics. Many entering the seminaries now have had their vocation nurtured in involvement with groups of young Catholics

---

143 See Colleen Carroll, *The New Faithful, Why Young Adults Are Embracing Christian Orthodoxy* (Chicago, 2002).
144 *Ibid.*, p. 3.
145 *Ibid.*, p. 15.

who are rediscovering their faith.

In the past, vocations were nurtured in the "triumvirate" of strong Catholic family life, parish and school. Today this is far less likely to be the defining element. The Catholic background that particularly animates the vocation is more likely to be a particular Catholic group or movement or a spiritual experience flowing from a Catholic activity. There is often a key person who has fired their faith or a particular moment when their faith is inspired. Some will speak of a defining experience which was a moment of discovery or enlightenment or of spiritual conversion.

Many seminarians have had their vocations nourished by the teaching and example of Pope John Paul II. Those who have attended World Youth Days will witness to the particular contribution that this experience of the Church and the opportunity to be in proximity to "JP2" has had on their faith and their vocation. Cardinal Ratzinger in his role as Prefect of the Congregation for the Doctrine of the Faith also has had a strong following among young people "in the know" about the Church, and his accession to the papacy has given them great heart for the future direction of the Church. These seminarians have read the writings of both in their pre-seminary days.

This new generation of seminarians are attracted to traditional expressions of the liturgy and devotions. Their liturgical tastes are clearly towards a faithful implementation of the liturgy with an orientation towards a more structured and reverent expression. They have little taste for many of the contemporary hymns and prefer the older traditional hymns. They like some Latin in the liturgy, and some of them lean towards to what is now referred to as "the Extraordinary Rite of the Roman Missal".[146]

The Rosary, Adoration of the Blessed Sacrament, veneration of the saints, and particular devotional practices currently in vogue (like Divine Mercy chaplets) form an integral part of their spiritual lives. They seriously seek to develop their spiritual life, and seek out reliable sources for their spiritual growth. They are well read on Catholic matters and are attracted by the traditional faith of the Church expressed in the lives of saints and authoritative teaching. Not only do they regularly go to confession, but often have a regular confessor to whom they turn for assistance in developing a stronger moral and spiritual life.

These seminarians are strong advocates of the traditional stance of the Church on matters like contraception, abortion, homosexuality and bioethics. They see themselves as going into society as advocates for the Church's teaching, and form their minds with apologetic arguments to defend their position. For these young men truth, objectively and clearly defined, is the passion of their lives. Their personal convictions echo Pope Benedict's insistence on the virtue of truth in the face of the "dictatorship of relativism"[147]. And they do not question priestly celibacy.

They have a distinct missionary spirit. They believe they have something to offer society. They want to be advocates of change proposing Catholic teaching to the world.

---

146 See the Apostolic Letter *Summorum Pontificum* issued as a Motu Proprio by Pope Benedict XVI, on 7 July 2007, on the celebration of the Roman Rite according to the Missal of 1962. In Article 1, the Pope explains, "The Roman Missal promulgated by Paul VI is the ordinary expression of the 'Lex orandi' (Law of prayer) of the Catholic Church of the Latin rite. Nonetheless, the Roman Missal promulgated by St. Pius V and reissued by Bl. John XXIII is to be considered as an extraordinary expression of that same 'Lex orandi,' and must be given due honour for its venerable and ancient usage. These two expressions of the Church's Lex orandi will in no any way lead to a division in the Church's 'Lex credendi' (Law of belief). They are, in fact two usages of the one Roman rite".

147 Mass, "Pro Eligendo Romano Pontifice" homily of his Eminence Cardinal Joseph Ratzinger, Dean of the College of Cardinals, 18 April 2005.

Priests for the future

George Weigel is a regular commentator on Church life. In his book, *God's Choice*,[148] which explores "Pope Benedict and the Future of the Catholic Church", he maps out what he considers as the way ahead for the Church. One issue he dwells on is the type of bishop needed for the Church in our time. He comments on the qualities needed to be witnessed in priests who could make good bishops. For our purposes we could consider his proposals as providing a consideration of what sort of priest is needed for these times. His checklist is given as follows:

> *Radical discipleship.* In his life and ministry does this priest manifest a personal conversion to Jesus Christ and a deliberate choice to abandon everything to follow Christ?

> *Evangelical energy.* Does this priest preach the Gospel with conviction and clarity? Can he make the Church's proposal to non-believers? With charity, can he instruct and, if necessary, admonish Catholics who have embraced teachings contrary to the Gospel and the teaching authority of the Church?

> *Pastoral effectiveness.* Has this priest ever been a pastor? Did the parish grow under his leadership? If his primary work has been as a professor in the seminary, did his students flourish under his tutelage?

> *Liturgical presence.* How does this priest celebrate the Mass, in concrete and specific terms? Does his liturgical ministry lead his people into a deeper experience of the paschal mystery of Jesus Christ, crucified and risen?

> *Personal example.* How many men have entered the seminary because of this priest's influence? How many

---

148 George Weigel, *God's Choice*, Harper Collins, 2005.

women have entered consecrated religious life because
of his influence? Does he encourage lay movements
of Catholic renewal and the development of popular
piety? In sum, is he a man who can call others to
holiness of life because he manifests holiness in his
own life?

The courage to be countercultural. Does this priest have the
strength of character and personality to make decisions
that will be unpopular with other priests and religious
because these decisions are faithful to the Church's
teaching and liturgical practices?

Theological literacy. Is this priest well read theologically?
Does he regard theology as an important part of his
vocation? Can he "translate" the best of the Church's
theology, ancient and contemporary into an idiom
accessible to his people?[149]

This checklist is a useful guide in the effort to clarify those defining
qualities that are needed in priests of today. They provide insight
into how the next generation of priests need to be formed. This
list marks out the qualities needed in priests who will be able to
contend with the challenges of this new millennium.

The Church of the third millennium.

We spoke earlier of the document, *Novo millennio ineunte*, issued by
Pope John Paul II at the beginning of the new millennium, which
spoke about "certain pastoral priorities" for achieving a pastoral
revitalisation in the Church. We saw that these proposals for what
is needed for the future are a clear affirmation of the vital role for
priestly ministry in the Church. The Pope sees the future of the
Church largely realised through the effective ministry of priests.

---

149 Weigel, *God's Choice*, pp. 250-251.

Priestly ministry lies at the heart of the life and mission of the Church. The effective ministry of priests ensures that the Church will continue to be strong and effective.

Duc in Altum **and** *Spe Salvi*

In the document, there was a phrase that seized the imagination of the Church as it entered the new millennium: *Duc in altum*, "put out into the deep". Pope John Paul was now seriously ageing. His body was failing him, yet his declaration to the Church at the dawn of a new millennium was full of hope and confidence for the future. He called on all Christians not to feel the weight of past failed effort – "we have toiled all night and caught nothing" – but to respond to a call by God to cast forth the nets in expectation for a great catch.

He called the Church to go "forward in hope". The reference to the story given in St Luke, chapter 5, was offered to the Church. The disciples had worked all night and caught nothing. Perhaps many who held great hopes for the future of the Church following Vatican II now feel disappointed. Their hopes have not been realised. Many can now feel tired, having, as they see it, laboured without great success. The voice of John Paul II cries out in the words of the Lord, "put out into the deep". The Gospel account tells us that obedience to this request of the Lord produced a great catch!

In a similar vein, Pope Benedict, in his measured and thoughtful way, proposed in his second encyclical, *Spe Salvi*, the theme of hope. This theme of hope is not without profound relevance at this point in history. In the face of a growing loss of faith, there has been an accompanying loss of hope. The rise in suicide is clear evidence of this. Choosing this theme, Pope Benedict puts the Christian contribution to modern society forward very clearly. In the opening thoughts of his teaching he says:

Here too we see as a distinguishing mark of Christians the fact that they have a future: it is not that they know the details of what awaits them, but they know in general terms that their life will not end in emptiness. Only when the future is certain as a positive reality does it become possible to live the present as well. So now we can say: Christianity was not only "good news"— the communication of a hitherto unknown content. In our language we would say: the Christian message was not only "informative" but "performative". That means: the Gospel is not merely a communication of things that can be known—it is one that makes things happen and is life-changing. The dark door of time, of the future, has been thrown open. The one who has hope lives differently; the one who hopes has been granted the gift of a new life.[150]

As Christians, as Catholics, as priests, we look at the world and the future with hope. This hope inspires us to be "performative". This hope urges us beyond a focus on ourselves and the immediate and gives an eternal perspective to what our lives are about. For priests it is the ultimate validation to their vocation. The meaning of priesthood is tied intimately to the transcendent – to the "last things". Priestly life and ministry rest firmly on this hope in a future, a transcendent future.

Pope John Paul has called us to put out into the deep and Pope Benedict has reminded us that our lives make ultimate sense in terms of the transcendent.

The Church, indeed the world, needs priests "after the heart of God". In every priest there is the mysterious outworking of the Grace of Ordination. Each priest is conscious in the depths of his being of a calling to be a priest in the name of Jesus Christ. Ordination has imprinted a character on his soul. Despite his fallen humanity there is a grace at work that constantly takes him beyond himself.

---

150 *Spe salvi*, n. 2.

"Cloud of Witnesses"

A priest, as he lives his priesthood, is caught up among the "cloud of witnesses" (Heb 12:1). These witnesses are the saints who are remembered in the liturgy. The priest in his daily Mass is presented with these saints over the course of the liturgical year. He commemorates their lives and comes to know them as he invokes their assistance and intercession through the prayers of the Mass. They are the faithful witnesses to Christ and to the Catholic faith. They are the Church now in heaven while we, who are the Church in pilgrimage on earth, look towards them with hope. We are reminded that our true homeland is in heaven.

In each Mass the congregation is invited to join them and the angels in their song of praise as they behold the glory of the Lord. We sing with them, "holy, holy, holy Lord...". In that moment our voices "blend with theirs"[151] as our minds are lifted up to be united with them. Here we taste the relationships that make up the Communion of Saints. Here we sense that bond that traverses time and situation. Earth and heaven are united. We are drawn beyond our grounding in this world.

A priest's daily life is one of being among his people on their pilgrimage through life. He walks alongside, often as brother and friend. He is there as fellow pilgrim and as guide. His ministry provides hope and encouragement. Each day in Mass he lifts up his eyes through the liturgy and is reminded of the goal. From the Mass he goes out among the people, bringing this hope and promise to them.

The priest lives his life in the sanctuary of the Catholic faith. As he lives the mystery of his calling daily he invokes the saints, inviting them to accompany him and his people with their prayers. The saints indeed "spur us on to victory".[152]

---

151 See *Roman Missal*, Preface of the Blessed Virgin Mary.

152 See *Roman Missal*, Preface of the holy men and women.

We all have our favourite saints. Priests have saints that are special to them. But priests have one saint who belongs to them in a special way. He is their patron: St John Vianney, the Cure of Ars, Patron Saint of Parish Priests.

This humble, dedicated pastor of souls exemplifies the nobility of the priesthood. His service in a small rural parish which occupied his whole priestly life is a witness to the ideals of the priesthood. He truly exemplifies one who is "after the heart of God".

Each priest and each seminarian can simply and humbly pray, "St John Vianney, pray for me!"

Bibliography

DOCUMENTS OF THE MAGISTERIUM

Vatican II

Constitution on the liturgy, *Sacrosanctum Concilium*, 4 December 1963
Constitution on the Church, *Lumen gentium*, 21 November 1964
Decree on the training of priests, *Optatam totius*, 28 October 1965
Constitution on divine revelation, *Dei Verbum*, 18 November 1965
Decree on the ministry and life of priests, *Presbyterorum ordinis*, 18 November 1965

Papal documents

Paul VI, Encyclical Letter, *Sacerdotalis caelibatus*, 24 June 1967
Apostolic Exhortation, *Evangeili nuntiandi*, 8 December 1975

John Paul II, Encyclical Letter, *Redemptor hominis*, 4 March 1979
Encyclical Letter, *Dives in misercordia*, 30 November 1980
Apostolic Letter, *Mulieris dignitatem*, 15 August 1988
Apostolic exhortation, *Christifideles laici*, 30 December 1988
Encyclical Letter, *Redemptoris missio*, 7 December 1990
Apostolic exhortation, *Pastores dabo vobis*, 25 March 1992
Encyclical Letter, *Veritatis splendor*, 6 August 1993
Apostolic Letter, *Ordinatio sacerdotalis*, 22 May 1994
Apostolic Letter, *Tertio millennio adveniente*, 10 November 1994
Encyclical Letter, *Evangelium vitae*, 25 March 1995
Apostolic Letter, *Dies Domini*, 31 May 1998
Apostolic Letter, *Novo millennio ineunte*, 6 January 2001
Encyclical Letter, *Ecclesia de Eucharistia*, 17 April 2003

Catechism of the Catholic Church, Dublin, 1994

Gift and mystery: on the fiftieth anniversary of my priestly ordination, London, 1996

Priests for the third millennium, Chicago, 1995 (series of addresses on priesthood during 1993)

Letters to my brother priests 1979-1999, Chicago, 2000

Benedict XVI, Encyclical Letter, *Deus Caritas Est*,
Encyclical Letter, *Spe Salvi*, 30 November 2007
Apostolic Letter *Summorum Pontificum*, 7 July 2007
Apostolic Exhortation, *Sacramentum Caritatis*, 22 February 2007

Other documents of the Magisterium

Congregation for the Doctrine of the Faith, *Instruction on certain aspects of "Theology of Liberation"*, 22 March 1986

Letter to the Bishops of the Catholic Church on the Pastoral Care of Homosexual persons, 1 October 1986

Letter to the Bishops of the Catholic Church on the collaboration of men and women in the Church and in the World, 31 May 2004

Doctrinal Note on some aspects of evangelisation, 6 October 2007

Congregation for Divine Worship and the Discipline of the Sacraments, *General instruction on the Liturgy of the Hours*, 11 April 1971
General instruction on the Roman Missal (Revised), 28 July 2000

Congregation for the Clergy, *Directory on the ministry and life of priests*, 31 January 1994

The priest and the third Christian millennium, Teacher of the Word, Minister of the Sacraments and Leader of the Community, 19 March 1999

Priest, Pastor and Leader of the Parish Community, 4 August 2002

Various congregations, *Instruction on certain questions regarding the collaboration of the non-ordained faithful in the sacred ministry of priests*, 15 August 1997

Pontifical Council for the Family, *Vademecum for confessors concerning some aspects of the morality of conjugal life*, 12 February 1997

OTHER BIBLIOGRAPHY

Benedict M. Ashley OP, *Living the truth in love: a biblical introduction to moral theology*, New York, 1996

St Alphonsus Liguori, *Dignity and duties of the priest*, New York, 1927

St Augustine of Hippo, *Confessions*, London, 2006
Rule of St Augustine, London, 1984

Jordan Aumann, *Spiritual theology*, London, 1985

Peter Brown, *Augustine of Hippo*, London, 1967

Colleen Carroll, *The New Faithful, Why Young Adults are embracing Christian Orthodoxy*, Chicago, 2002

St John Chrysostom, *On the priesthood: a treatise*, Westminster MD, 1943

James Coriden, *The Parish in Catholic Tradition*, New Jersey, 1997

Avery Dulles, *The priestly office: a theological reflection*, New York, 1997

A. Flannery, (ed), *Vatican Council II: the conciliar and post conciliar documents*, Dublin, 1981

Stefan Heid, *Celibacy in the early Church*, San Francisco, 2001

Marcial Maciel, *Integral Formation of Catholic Priests*, 1998

Thomas J. McGovern, *Priestly celibacy today,* Dublin and Chicago, 1998
Priestly Identity, Dublin, 2002 Servais Pinckaers,
The sources of Christian ethics, Edinburgh, 1995
Morality, the Catholic View, South Bend, 2001

Dermot Power, *A Spiritual Theology of the Priesthood*, Edinburgh, 1998

Joseph Ratzinger, *The Ratzinger Report, Joseph Cardinal Ratzinger with Vittorio Messori*, San Francisco, 1985

'The ministry and life of priests', *Homiletic and Pastoral Review*,
    August-September 1997
    The spirit of the liturgy, San Francisco, 2000

Michael Rose, *Goodbye, Good Men*, Cincinnati, 2002

Alfons M. Stickler, *The case for clerical celibacy: its historical development
    and theological foundations*, San Francisco, 1995

Peter Stravinskas, ed. *Priestly Celibacy*, 2001

Luc Verheijen *Saint Augustine, Monk, Priest, Bishop,* Pennsylvannia, 1978

George Weigel, *The Courage to be Catholic*, Washington, 2002
    God's Choice, New York, 2005

About The Author

Most Rev Julian Porteous BTheol DD VG was born in Sydney in 1949. He was ordained a priest for the Archdiocese of Sydney in 1974. Bishop Porteous served as Assistant Priest in a number of parishes, before being appointed a Parish Priest. He has been actively involved in evangelisation, particularly among young people. He has been an advocate of the New Evangelisation called for by Pope John Paul II. He was appointed Rector of the Seminary of the Good Shepherd, Sydney, in January 2002 and served in this role until the end of 2008. In his role as Rector he focussed on the formation of priests for the particular circumstances of the Church at the beginning of the new millennium. Pope John Paul II named him Auxiliary Bishop of Sydney in July 2003. Bishop Porteous has published a number of books including, *St Brendan's, a Journey: The Story of an Australian Catholic Parish 1898 –1998"* (1997); *The New Evangelisation, Developing Evangelical Preaching* (Connor Court Publishing, 2008).